The Doubtful Heir by James Shirley

A TRAGI-COMEDIE. As it was Acted at the private House in Black Fryers

James Shirley was born in London in September 1596.

His education was through a collection of England's finest establishments: Merchant Taylors' School, London, St John's College, Oxford, and St Catharine's College, Cambridge, where he took his B.A. degree in approximately 1618.

He first published in 1618, a poem entitled Echo, or the Unfortunate Lovers.

As with many artists of this period full details of his life and career are not recorded. Sources say that after graduating he became "a minister of God's word in or near St Albans." A conversion to the Catholic faith enabled him to become master of St Albans School from 1623–25.

He wrote his first play, Love Tricks, or the School of Complement, which was licensed on February 10th, 1625. From the given date it would seem he wrote this whilst at St Albans but, after its production, he moved to London and to live in Gray's Inn.

For the next two decades, he would write prolifically and with great quality, across a spectrum of thirty plays; through tragedies and comedies to tragicomedies as well as several books of poetry. Unfortunately, his talents were left to wither when Parliament passed the Puritan edict in 1642, forbidding all stage plays and closing the theatres.

Most of his early plays were performed by Queen Henrietta's Men, the acting company for which Shirley was engaged as house dramatist.

Shirley's sympathies lay with the King in battles with Parliament and he received marks of special favor from the Queen.

He made a bitter attack on William Prynne, who had attacked the stage in Histriomastix, and, when in 1634 a special masque was presented at Whitehall by the gentlemen of the Inns of Court as a practical reply to Prynne, Shirley wrote the text—The Triumph of Peace.

Shirley spent the years 1636 to 1640 in Ireland, under the patronage of the Earl of Kildare. Several of his plays were produced by his friend John Ogilby in Dublin in the first ever constructed Irish theatre; The Werburgh Street Theatre. During his years in Dublin he wrote The Doubtful Heir, The Royal Master, The Constant Maid, and St. Patrick for Ireland.

In his absence from London, Queen Henrietta's Men sold off a dozen of his plays to the stationers, who naturally, enough published them. When Shirley returned to London in 1640, he finished with the Queen Henrietta's company and his final plays in London were acted by the King's Men.

On the outbreak of the English Civil War Shirley served with the Earl of Newcastle. However when the King's fortunes began to decline he returned to London. There his friend Thomas Stanley gave him help and thereafter Shirley supported himself in the main by teaching and publishing some educational works under the Commonwealth. In addition to these he published during the period of dramatic eclipse four small volumes of poems and plays, in 1646, 1653, 1655, and 1659.

It is said that he was "a drudge" for John Ogilby in his translations of Homer's Iliad and the Odyssey, and survived into the reign of Charles II, but, though some of his comedies were revived, his days as a playwright were over.

His death, at age seventy, along with that of his wife, in 1666, is described as one of fright and exposure due to the Great Fire of London which had raged through parts of London from September 2nd to the 5th.

He was buried at St Giles in the Fields, in London, on October 29th, 1666.

Index of Contents
To the Most Worthily Honored Sir Edmund Bowier
DRAMATIS PERSONAE
SCENE - Murcia
PROLOGUE
THE DOUBTFUL HEIR
ACT I
SCENE I - The Palace
ACT II
SCENE I - The Palace
SCENE II - A Street
SCENE III - A Prison
SCENE IV - A Court of Justice
ACT III
SCENE I - The Palace. A Garden
ACT IV
SCENE I - An Apartment in the Palace
SCENE II - The Palace. The Queen's Apartment
ACT V
SCENE I - The Palace
SCENE II - A Prison
SCENE III - Near the Palace
SCENE IV - An Apartment in the Palace
EPILOGUE
JAMES SHIRLEY – A CONCISE BIBLIOGRAPHY

To the Most Worthily Honored Sir Edmund Bowier

SIR,

Many years are vanished, and a period, not onely of the Scene, but more considerable revolutions have pass'd, since I had the happiness to be first known to you. I read excellent Characters of you, when you writ but a small Letter, and though my observations, like seeds, were not cherished (by the fault of time) to a maturity, yet they begat in me such great respect to your person, then budding with honour, and expectation, that now after so long absence, I find them not extinguished; and howsoever at the first complexion, I may appear bold, in this hasty interruption, yet your candour will be so far in my defence, that I have presumed thus, rather to let you know I can still honour you, than unsatisfie my self, by neglecting the first opportunity of presenting my service. Sir, it is a piece, which perhaps you have seen in the active representment; the estimation it gained from thence, will be short of that grace it shall derive from your acceptance, by which you will shew, how still you dare retain your nobleness, and by renewing your smile upon me, encourage me to write my self

Your humble Servant,
JAMES SHIRLEY.

DRAMATIS PERSONAE
Leonario. Prince of Arragon
Ferdinand, King of Murcia
Rodriguez   }
Ernesto   } Noblemen attending on the Court
Leandro   }
Alfonso, Father to Rosania
Olivia, supposed Queen of Murcia
Rosania, Alfonso's, Daughter
Violinda
Captain
Four Citizens (as Lieutenant, Ancient etc)
Courtier
Officers
Souldiers
Keeper of a Prison

SCENE

Murcia.

PROLOGUE

All that the Prologue comes for, is to say,
Our Author did not calculate this Play
For this Meridian; the Banckside, he knows,
Are far more skilfull at the Ebbes and flows

Of water, than of wit, he did not mean
For the elevation of your poles, this scene.
No shews, no dance, and what you most delight in,
Grave understanders, here's no target fighting
Upon the Stage, all work or Cutlers barr'd,
No bawdery, nor no Ballets; this goes hard;
But language clean, and what affects you not,
Without impossibilities the Plot;
No clown, no squibs, no Devil in't; oh now
You Squirrels that want Nuts, what will you do?
Pray do not crack the benches; and we may
Hereafter fit your Palats with a Play:
But you that can contract your selves, and sit
As you were now in the Black-Fryers pit;
And will not deaf us, with leud noise and tongues,
Because we have no Heart to break our Lungs,
Will pardon our vast Stage, and not disgrace
This Play, meant for your persons, not the place.

THE DOUBTFUL HEIR

ACT I

SCENE I

The Palace

Enter **RODRIGUEZ** and **ERNESTO**.

RODRIGUEZ
This turn was not expected, Prince Leonario
Is much perplext.

ERNESTO
I cannot blame his Highness,
So neer an expectation of a blessing,
To be thus crost.

RODRIGUEZ
The Day of Marriage sef,
With the applausive Vote of both the Kingdoms,
By an unlookt for War to be put of,
Would vex a royall spleen.

ERNESTO
'Tis but deferr'd.

RODRIGUEZ
I doe not like the hope on't.

ERNESTO
I pittie
The Princely lover, worthy (without blemish
To the excelling virtues of the Queen)
Of as much goodness as her sex contains,
So Noble in his Nature, Active, bountiful
Discreet, and valiant, if we may believe
What his young fame profers to every knowledge.

RODRIGUEZ
This character is not flattery, and yet
The Queen our Mistriss is not lost in this
Just praise of him.

ERNESTO
I have no thought so Impious,
My dutie never taught me to commend
But to obey, her Virgin sweetness makes me
Her just admirer but when I observe
Her prudent manage of the State, a strength
Would become many years, her pious Laws,
But that without example, made to advance
Her sexes Chastitie, I forget all
Beside worth praise, though every least of her
Desert would ask a volume. 'Tis his Excellence.

[Enter **LEONARIO**, **CAPTAIN**.

RODRIGUEZ
Ther's one not sorry for these Wars.

ERNESTO
'Tis his
Profession; Souldiers batten in a Tempest.

RODRIGUEZ
And he deserves employment; yet I think
Hee'l never purchase with his pay.

LEONARIO
Be confident;
Your worth will plead alone; the Queen expects me.

[Exit **LEONARIO**

CAPTAIN
Your Highness humble creature;—so, ther's hope yet
After a time of ease, and surfet, we
May cure our selves by letting others Blood.
My Noble Lords.

ERNESTO
'Morrow Captain, you look blith, and bright.

CAPTAIN
I'l put my Sword to scowring that shall shine.
I thank Heaven my prayers are heard.

RODRIGUEZ
What prayers?

CAPTAIN
That honest men may cut knaves throats, and bid
Defiance to the Hangman; Musk, and Civet
Have too long stifled us, ther's no recovery
Without the smell of Gunpowder.

[Enter two **CITIZENS**.

ERNESTO
But Captain—

1ST CITIZEN
'Tis he, we must not lose him,

2ND CITIZEN
He has credit with the Lords it seems.

1ST CITIZEN
He has spied us.

CAPTAIN
My honest friends, welcome to Court. My Lords
Pray grace these honest Gentlemen, they will
Deserve to kiss your Hands.

1ST CITIZEN
Our business
Is to you Captain.

CAPTAIN
Doe you think what these brace of Baboons come for?

RODRIGUEZ
Not I.

CAPTAIN
By this day for mony, moneys that I owe 'em.

ERNESTO
Is't possible?

CAPTAIN
I ha' mov'd your sute Gentlemen.

1ST CITIZEN
What sute?

CAPTAIN
Touching the Masque. Which you two in the name
Of the whole City, offer'd to present
At the Town charges to congratulate
The Queens intended Marriage; I know
This Egge was long a hatching, and expected,
But that your Heads could not agree, they being
Of severall sizes, some upon the shoulders
Of your long-winded Officers, whose purse
Was made of the Leather with their conscience.

1ST CITIZEN
Does he talk to us of a Masque?

2ND CITIZEN
Good Captain put your Masque off, and give us.
The money that you owe us.

CAPTAIN
Was't not meant nobly?
But you my good Lords know how much
The Queen and Prince are sorry, that so rare
A President of their duty should not be
Upon record; this villanous War distracts
All civill mirth, but you will be remembred.

1ST CITIZEN
We know not what you mean, we have no anticks
In agitation; if your Captain-ship
Will pay your debts so; there is Law and courses
To be taken, and you will find that Justice
Can deal Sir with the Sword as well as Ballance.

CAPTAIN
The Puppys talk Philosophy; nay then
I must be plain, would I could tice 'em to
A little treason, they I ner hang for felony.
Why, whither doe you think I am going now?

1ST CITIZEN
We care not whither, so you pay us first.

CAPTAIN
Let their own Fathers swing, so they have money.

2ND CITIZEN
May be you are going to the Wars.

CAPTAIN
Yes Mongrels,
To fight for your chamlet Faces, while you stay at home
And catch the cramp with telling money,
Putting your Guts to Pension every Day,
And roots, untill the wind cry out agen you,
And with your belching backwards stifle Men
That walk the Street, until the Air be purg'd;
Must we Eat Bullets without Butter, Whelps?
Have our Throats cut, or drop like Sheep by'th' hundred,
O' the rot, to buy your Peace you boding Screechowls?
And ha' your consciences so course a Nap
To aske money of us?

1ST CITIZEN
You had the conscience
To take up our commodities.

CAPTAIN
Reason good;
Should I go naked leeches?

2ND CITIZEN
No but there is reason
That you should pay good Captain for your warmth.

CAPTAIN
Pay you? for what? for Cloaths, such things as these?
Your tribe is bound to keep us.

1ST CITIZEN
How?

CAPTAIN
Yes, and desire us to accept your wares,
To recompence our sufferings; 'tis we,
'Tis we that keep your Worships warm and living,
By Marching, Fasting, Fighting and a thousand
Dangers. (you o'r grown moths) you that love gold,
And wo'not take an Angell sent from Heaven
Unless you weigh him, you that spend the Day
In looking o'r your debt—Book, and at Night
Can lap and lecher in your Feather Beds,
Then snort, and dream of fourscore in the hundred,
Afraid of nothing but the Gout, or what
Is a more just reward for your hard hearts
The stone, which puts you to the charge of Physick
To make you piss out your last Usurers Gallon,
Or of a Surgeon, to cut you for
The Pebbles which (if you survive Incission)
You keep in penny Boxes, like deer reliques,
And shew your friends, when you intend to visit 'em.
And beg a Dinner.

ERNESTO
Let not passion
Make you too much abuse their quality;
The City does contain brave fellows Captain,
As generous, as bountifull, discreet,
And valiant too, as any boast themselves
In Court or Camp.

CAPTAIN
I grant you my good Lord,
And honour all the Noble souls within it,
But these are walking sicknesses, not Citizens;
Two such prodigious things with crooked consciences,
Though Young, yet Old in Usury—

2ND CITIZEN
All this Captain
Wo 'not pay us our money, which we must
Have or Petition for to your disgrace.

CAPTAIN
Well since there is no remedy, will you take
These two Noblemens words for what I owe you?

1ST CITIZEN
Withall our Hearts.

RODRIGUEZ
That bargain is to make.

ERNESTO
Good Captain, at this time you may excuse us,

CAPTAIN
Why, doe your Lordships think I'd let you suffer,
Come, y'ar my honourable friends; pass, pass
Your word, Ile pay the mony; hang 'em dottrels
Ile not be beholding to 'em.

RODRIGUEZ
We had rather you should good Captain.

CAPTAIN
No,—come hither Capons
Will money content you; shall I walk the Street
Without a Head ake, with your bawling for
The debt when I ha' paid you?

2ND CITIZEN
'Tis but reason.

CAPTAIN
I'l fetch you money presently,—you may follow
If you please, but these Noblemen shall see
And witness what I pay you, I'l not trust
Your Memorandums.

1ST CITIZEN
Withall our Hearts Sir.

2ND CITIZEN
We desire no more.

CAPTAIN
I'l wait on you again.

[Exeunt **CAPTAIN** and **CITIZENS**.

[Enter **LEANDRO**, reading a Paper.

RODRIGUEZ
Fortune de la guerre.
My Lord Leandro? what papers that
He so intentively peruses?

LEANDRO
I like it, and could willingly allow
The change; the Queen grows mighty in her spirit,
And this match with the Prince, would swell her State
Too much; my Lords.

RODRIGUEZ
We are yours.

LEANDRO
See what dangerous Papers have been scatter'd
To wound the Title of our Royall Mistriss;
My servant brought me this; our Enemie
Who calls himself Prince Ferdinand would fain
Have us believe him Cosen to the Queen,
She an usurper of his Crown.

ERNESTO
We all know him dead.

RODRIGUEZ
I'm sure I did attend his Funeral.

LEANDRO
I think I waited too.

ERNESTO
This paper sayes he was conveyd away,
And so escap'd his Uncles cruelty.
To whose protection he was left an Infant;
He dying we translated our obedience
To his Daughter, now our Queen.

RODRIGUEZ
Here's an Impostor.

LEANDRO
Heaven aid the Innocent say I; he has
Valencias aid and comes not to Invite
But force a resignation; I wish things
Were calm agen.

ERNESTO
Prince Leonario, if she prosper not,
Is like to be a loser too.

LEANDRO

For him
It matters not, we have more to think on now,
Than love and complement.

RODRIGUEZ
I thought he would be General
'Gainst this pretended Ferdinand.

LEANDRO
What else?
Her sweet Heart that gives Cupid in his crest.
Alas! there needs no art, nor strength of War
To advance her cause Justice will fight for her
I'th' Clouds, and victory sent from Heaven, without
Her souldiers sweat, will gloriously descend
To Crown his Head with Laurell.

ERNESTO
May it prove so.

LEANDRO
I could say things would stagger your belief,
But I forgot the Queen sent for me; to
You both a servant—

[Exit.

ERNESTO
I do not like my Lord Leandros winding,
He has been faithful.

RODRIGUEZ
Alwaies honourable. The Queen.

[Enter **QUEEN, LEONARIO, CAPTAIN, LEANDRO, VIOLINDA, ATTENDANTS, LADIES, GENTLEMEN**.

LEONARIO
I take this as the greatest honour Madam
You could confer; my name is young in War,
But my affection to your royall person,
Arm'd with the virtue of your cause, shall make me
Doe something worth your name.

QUEEN
'Twas your request,
Nor could we place our chief command, but where
'Tis equald with your Interest in us
And your own merit.

LEONARIO
Sure my Stars did mean
This way to make you know, how much my heart
Dares in your service; and if Ferdinand,
For so he calls himself, possess a soul
Above the vulgar making, we shall spare
The Blood of many, and conclude the War
In single opposition.

LEANDRO
With your Highness pardon,
It not becomes you should Engage your Person,
And so great a cause so dangerously;
It will be too much honor to th' Impostor,
And in the supposition of the World,
A strength to his pretence, to bring your Birth
So low, to humble both your self and fortunes
To his unworthy Level; a thing grown
Up in the Night. a Meteor hanging in
The Air prodigiously, fed with vapor, and
Black Influence, ambitious to deceive
The World, and challenge kindred with the Stars;
It is too great a venture Sir.

ERNESTO
Since there must be a War
Let the armies meet in Battail, theres more hope
After the worst to reinforce, and prosper,
Than when the kingdoms put upon one stake,
And one Mans chance to assure it.

QUEEN
I allow
Your Counsell Lords; but have more argument
Convincing me, not to run such a hazard
Of what must make Olivia rich hereafter;
A kingdoms loss may be repair'd, but your
Life made a Sacrifice to tyrant War,
May find a welcome to the other shades,
But no tears can Invite you back, to share,
Or grief, or Joy with me; Ile have no Duell.

LEONARIO
'Tis a command, and my obedience
Shall meet it, though I fear 'twill be a sin
To be too carefull of my self but I
Shall still remember I am your Souldier,

And this consider'd shall not make me rash,
But wisely teach me to deserve this title
Which lives but in your honour.

QUEEN
I'l pray for you.
And not so much for what concerns the State,
As what your merit hath already gain'd
Upon my Heart.

RODRIGUEZ
Blessings upon 'em both,
A curse upon these Wars, that spoil their mirth.

QUEEN
My Lord Leandro.

LEONARIO
Ther's your Commission Captain, I suppose
You have found wayes to empty your Exchequer.

CAPTAIN
My Baggs are not brimfull my Lord. I have
Defalk'd, and made an ebbe for Wine, and Women,
And other things that keep poor men alive
To doe their country service.

LEONARIO
Please you walk
With this Gentleman Captain he shall pay you
Five hundred pieces that I owe you.

CAPTAIN
Me, your Grace owes me nothing,

LEONARIO
I could not pay the debt in better time Sir.

CAPTAIN
Umh! I will take the money, and allow the miracle.

[Exit **CAPTAIN & GENTLEMAN**.

ERNESTO
Did you observe the Princes nobleness?
Although the act become him. Yet the manner
Takes me especially, Heaven preserve the Captain
From being Mad.

LEONARIO
I prosper in your Vote,
But shall I Madam, if that power, which Crowns
With victory, guides me with fair success
In this your War, and triumph smile upon us,
Shall I at my return have that reward
My soul next Heaven affects? shall no delay
(Colder than Frost to lovers blood,) afflict
My expectation of our Marriage?
Although to doubt this be a sin, yet where
The ambition is so Just. I shall but right
My Heart, to have it oft assur'd nor can
It make your eye less rich in smiles, when 'tis
Only my love Encourages me to make
The busie harmless question.

QUEEN
It does please me,
Nor can you ask so often, as I have
A cheerfulness to answer, that I love you,
And have propounded nothing dearer to me,
Than that which perfects chast affection,
And chains two Hearts; the Priest with sadness will
Expect you safe agen, but from this War
When you return, he shall not in his Register
Of Lovers, find one with more wing hath met
The bosom of her friend, than glad Olivia
To make one soul with you.

LEONARIO
I have enough,
And thirst for action in the Field, from whence
I will bring Harvest home, or leave my self,
Happy in life or death to doe you service.

[Exit **QUEEN, LEONARIO, LEANDRO, LADIES, ATTENDANTS**.

RODRIGUEZ
Well, I'm afraid if Hymen should set up
His Tapers now, they would not last to light
His Priest, at their return to say his Office.

ERNESTO
Hope fairly.

RODRIGUEZ
I allow his spirit, but

The Prince hath not been practis'd in
The School of War, where stratagems prevail
Above all personall resolution.

ERNESTO
He cannot want fit counsell to direct
His early valour, besides
Ferdinand by computation as young as he

[Enter **CAPTAIN**, followed by two **CITIZENS**, and a **SOULDIER**.

May poize the scale. See, the Captain.

1ST CITIZEN
We alwaies thought you Noble, and we hope
You'l take no offence, that our occasions
Prevail'd above our modestie.

CAPTAIN
I know
You two are very modest; well I'm glad
I am furnish'd for you: my good Lords I must
Intreat you to be witnesses of what money
I pay these Gentlemen, that have trusted me.

2ND CITIZEN
And will agen; command our Shops.

CAPTAIN
No, sit there, and starve,
Or if you like it better take a swing
At your own sign Post.

ERNESTO
Good words Captain.

CAPTAIN
They expect good money, and both good are too much.

1ST CITIZEN
We always lov'd you.

2ND CITIZEN
And doe so still most virtuously.

CAPTAIN
It does appear.

1ST CITIZEN
And you shall find us ready—

CAPTAIN
I'll make but one fair motion, it will be
Sufficient tryall of your honestie;
I have five hundred pounds, you see me tell it,
Faith make it up a thousand 'twixt you both
Till I come back, you will be Aldermen.

1ST CITIZEN
Ne'r a whit the sooner.

2ND CITIZEN
Alas Sir, if it were at another time—

1ST CITIZEN
Hereafter, upon good occasion you shall find—

CAPTAIN
You both i'th' Pillorie, for selling Copper
Lace by a wrong name; well ther's no remedy,
I'll keep my word; the money's ready for you.

1ST CITIZEN
You are noble Captain.

2ND CITIZEN
May you kill all the Queens Enemies.

CAPTAIN
You would not scape,
That Cosen her liege people every day, then.

2ND CITIZEN
This payment Captain will come most seasonably.

1ST CITIZEN
And doe us as much good, as you had given us
The sum twice told, another time.

CAPTAIN
Before
These Noblemen, have you such want
As you profess? you have no Wives nor Children.

1ST CITIZEN
I protest upon my credit, I am to pay

This day two hundred pound, or be indanger'd
To an arrest.

2ND CITIZEN
And I must goe to Prison
If before Sun-set—

CAPTAIN
Then 'twill doe you a pleasure.

BOTH CITIZENS
Above expression.

CAPTAIN
Heres twelve pence a piece for you y'ar fit Men

[Gives them money.

To serve the Queen:

BOTH CITIZENS
How Captain?

CAPTAIN
Why in the Wars, choose either Pike or Musket,
You shall have that favour.

BOTH CITIZENS
We are both undone.

LORDS
Ha, ha, but will you use 'em so?

CAPTAIN
Ha' they not ready mony? why d'ee stare?
No thanks for my protection?

BOTH CITIZENS
Protection?

CAPTAIN
Did you not protest you should to prison else?
Why you unthankful sons of false light, Sergeant
Take 'em to their Rendevous

1ST CITIZEN
Captain, a word-we are content—

CAPTAIN
I'm glad on't, Why d'ee stay then.

1ST CITIZEN
To abate half our money.

2ND CITIZEN
All, all good Captain, he shall have all, rather
Than be sent a souldiering; d'ee know what 'tis?
'Tis no Artillery Garden, where you come off
With as you were [to **1ST CITIZEN**].

RODRIGUEZ
This was his Project.

CAPTAIN
Umph! You will forgive me both your debts?

2ND CITIZEN
And pray Heaven to forgive you too.

CAPTAIN
My Lords, bear witness,
These two would bribe me to abuse the Queen
And the present service, is this less then Treason?

BOTH CITIZENS
Oh.

ERNESTO
Nay, nay Captain.

CAPTAIN
There are not two more able Men i'th' Army,
I mean for bulk; ram me into a Cannon
If you shall buy your selves with your estates
From this Imployment; Il not cosen you,
Your mony is good debt still, you may live,
And aske me for't agen, and I may pay you.

RODRIGUEZ
But shall they serve indeed?

CAPTAIN
That's at their perill
When they come to 'th, field, but goe they shall,
And they were my Cosen-germans.

BOTH CITIZENS
Good my Lord speak for us.

CAPTAIN
You doe not know my Lords, but a little suffering
May save their souls, and teach 'em, if they come
Off, with a quarter of their limbs, compassion
To other Men, that venter their lives for 'em,
Their consciences are tough, and must be suppled,
When they shall fast, and march ten months in armor,
Sometimes through Rivers, sometimes over Mountains,
And not have straw at Night, to keep their Breech
From growing to the Earth, in storms, in heats;
When they have felt the softness of a trench
Thigh deep in water, and their dung to fatten it;
When they shall see no meat within a month,
But chaw their Match like Liquorish, and digest
The Bark of trees like Sallads in the Summer;
When they shall live to think theres no such thing
In Nature as a thirst, and wonder why
A Taylor was created; when they have
As much in ready shot, within their flesh,
As would set up a Plummer, or repair
A Church with Lead, beside ten thousand more
Afflictions, which they are sure to find,
They may have Christianitie, and not put
A Souldier to the payment of his debts.

RODRIGUEZ
'Tis a Mad Captain, come my Lord lets leave him.

[Exit **LORDS**.

CAPTAIN
You shall have time and place to send for mony,
Or make your Wils; set on, who knows but you
Hereafter may be honest, and prove Captains;
You may have preferment in the Wars for money,
And so my Gentle Creditors, march on.

[Exeunt.

ACT II

SCENE I

The Palace.

[Enter **LEANDRO** with Letters.

LEANDRO
The hope, and care of many years, are in
One day destroy'd; hath Heaven no stroke in War?
Or is old providence asleep? Leonario
Is coming home with victorie, and brings
Young Ferdinand, whom I expected to
Salute a King, his Prisoner, and the Queen
With her new Conqueror, glorious in the spoils,
By putting out this light, will mix their beams
And burn our eyes out with their shine; there is
No talk but of this triumph, and the people
Whom I by art and secret murmurs had
Made doubtful at the first noise of this Conquest,
As they had borrowed souls from fear, and folly,
Adore the rising Star, and in the praise
Of him and his great fate, wonder that Heaven
Should hold a Sun, and he so bright; nor with
This flattery content, but they condemn,
(As low as all their sins shall one day them)
Him whom the chance of War hath made a Prisoner.
There is no trust to policy or time,
The things of State are whirld by destinie,
To meet their period, Art cannot repair 'em.

[Enter **SERVANT**.

SERVANT
My Lord, the Queen hath sent for you,
She is going forth to meet the Prince, and hath
Commanded none be wanting to attend
With all the State that may become here to
Congratulate the triumph now brought home.

LEANDRO
I shall obey. I must attend this glorie;
It is not safe to wear a brow, but what
The Queens example first forms into smile.
I here contract my knowledge, and seclude
My wishes, since they prosper not. I am
Her Chancelor as great Offices, and high
Employments, do expose us to most danger,
They oft teach those possess 'em a State-wisdom,
And by Inherent virtues of the place,
Our fear to lose, makes us secure our selves,

By art more often, than by conscience;
But I may be indangered to suspition;
I like not things; but I delay my attendance.

[Exit.

SCENE II

A Street.

[Enter **CAPTAIN**, and two **CITIZENS**, dressed, the one as a Lieutenant, the other as an **ANCIENT** and followed by **SOULDIERS**.

CAPTAIN
Lieutenant.

LIEUTENANT
Captain.

CAPTAIN
Ancient, what think you of the Wars now?

ANCIENT
We are come off with Honour.

LIEUTENANT
And our Limbs, Captain.

CAPTAIN
Is that all? who made you a Lieutenant?
And you Ancient? these titles were not born w'e,
You did not wear these Buffs and Feathers in
The memorie of Man, when you receiv'd
The binding twelve-pence, it was otherwise.

ANCIENT
But you receiv'd, if you remember Captain,
Beside what we releast in honest debt
Sums for this great Instalment, we ha' paid
I take it for our names.

CAPTAIN
And it became you,
Now you are Gentlemen my Comrades of honor,
And I dare walk and drink at Taverns w'e,
Your oaths become you now, and your splay feet;

You look'd before like Magots, City Worms,
I ha' made you both brave fellows, fellows to Knights.
You may be Squires to Ladies too.

ANCIENT
I think so.

CAPTAIN
We are all now of a trade,
For Mars is Master of our Companie,
Our Shop is the Field, Resolution our Stock,
Honour our Purchase, and Fire and Sword
The Tools we work withall.

LIEUTENANT
But now the Wars are done, I think
We may shut up our Shop, there is no more
Pay, is there?

CAPTAIN
Pox upon you; I see your souls bleat after
Profit still, a bullet in the right place would
Ha' knock'd out this humour of getting mony;
But fear not, though you come off with more
Limbs than you deserve, you shall have pay.

ANCIENT
Shall we, and not be troubled to fight for't?

CAPTAIN
Yes, it will be necessary you fight, you will
Ha' your throats cut else, and be sent off like Sheep,
Doe not fear payment here be Mandrakes,
That will rore, and cudgell you to your hearts content,
You sha'not walk the Screets now you are
Officers without a quarrell: pay enough.

LIEUTENANT
A Man had as good be no Lieutenant, as be
Beaten when he comes home what think you Ancient?

ANCIENT
For my part I can indure beating as well
As another, if that be all.

CAPTAIN
Will you to your Shops agen?

ANCIENT
I have no mind to Woosted Stockings agen,
And Shoos that Shine, I would were colours still.

CAPTAIN
Well said Ancient, come I'l take your fears off;
Doe not confess you are a Lieutenant, or you an
Ancient, and no man will quarrel w'ee, you
Shall be as secure as Chrysome Children.

LIEUTENANT
Shall we? they shall rack me e'r Ile confess I am
A Lieutenant or ever see the Wars.

ANCIENT
Or I an Ancient. Ile tak't upon my death
I was never a Souldier in my life.

CAPTAIN
'Tis well done; now because I love you,
And see you have an Itch after honour, so
It may come without blows, Let me advise you,
You have moneys at command.

LIEUTENANT
And good debts too.

CAPTAIN
You shall both turn Courtiers.

ANCIENT
Shall we?

CAPTAIN
I say't; for if my phisnomy deceive me not,
You two are born to be—

BOTH
What?

CAPTAIN
Coxbombs. I'l help to make you too;
You shall presently kiss the Queens hand;
You have moneys you say, You shall never turn
To your vomit of small Wares. I have friends
At Court, you may in time be great; And when I come
With a Petition to your honors, for moneys in arrear,
Or knocking out some rascals brains, such as you were

When you wore a girt under your chops, you two
May stand between me and the Gallows.

ANCIENT
Hang us if we do not.

CAPTAIN
You shall buy places presently. But stay,
Have you a minde to be Officers to the Queen
In ordinary, or extraordinary?

ANCIENT
Extraordinary by all means.

LIEUTENANT
We scorn to be ordinary Courtiers.

CAPTAIN
I commend your judgement, that will be more
Chargeable: But—

ANCIENT
Hang't, we'l finde money enough, but I
Resolve to be extraordinary.

CAPTAIN
I'l bring you to a Court-Merchant presently;
You will get infinite estates.

BOTH
A ha Captain.

CAPTAIN
And so command the Ladies, if you be bountiful.

BOTH
A ha Boy.

CAPTAIN
For I know you do love Wenches;
You will have all the business and the Country
Come tumbling in upon you like the tide,
After a moneth: You must keep twenty men
Between you, night and day to tell your money.
Oh 'tis unknown what will become on you,
If you be ruled, and take this course: Had I
Moneys like you, I would be—

LIEUTENANT
Come, we will lend thee moneys too hereafter.

CAPTAIN
Will you, come on, no more Lieutenant now.
Nor Ancient.

ANCIENT
Do ye think we long to be beaten.

[Exeunt.

SCENE III

A Prison

[Enter **FERDINAND**, and **ROSANIA** disguised like a Page.

ROSANIA
Pray do not grieve for me, I have a heart
That can for your sake suffer more; and when
The tyranny of your fate calls me to die,
I can as willingly resign my breath,
As go to sleep.

FERDINAND
Can I hear this Rosania
Without a fresh wound? That thy love to me
Should be so ill rewarded, th'ast engag'd
Thy self too much already; 'tis within
Thy will, yet to be safe, reveal thy self,
Throw of the cloud that doth eclipse that brightness,
And they will court thy person, and be proud
With all becoming-honor to receive thee,
No fear shall rob thy cheek of her chaste blood.
Oh leave me to my own Stars, and expect
What ere become of wretched Ferdinand,
A happy fate.

ROSANIA
Your Councel is unkinde,
This language would become your charity
To a stranger, but my Interest is more
In thee, then thus with words to be sent off;
Our vows have made us one, nor can the names
Of Father, Countrey, or what can be dear

In Nature, bribe one thought to wish my self
In Heaven without thy company; it were poor then
To leave thee here. Then by thy faith I charge thee,
By this—the first and last seal of our love.

[Kisses him.

By all our promises, when we did flatter
Our selves, and in our fancy took the world
A pieces, and collected what did like
Us best, to make us a new paradise,
By that, the nob est ornament of thy soul,
Thy honor, I conjure thee, let me still
Be undiscovered; What will it avail
To leave me, whom thou lovest, and walk alone
Sad pilgrim to another world? We will
Converse in soul and shoot like Stars, whose Beams
Are twisted, and make bright the sullen Groves
Of Lovers as we pass.

FERDINAND
These are but dreams
Of happiness, be wise Rosania,
Thy love is not a friend to make thee miserable,
Society in death, where we affect,
But multiplies our grief; Live thou, Oh live.
And if thou hast a tear, when I am dead,
But drop it to my memory, it shall
More precious then embalming dwell upon me,
And keep my ashes pure, my spirit shall
At the same instant in some innocent shape
Descend upon that earth thou hast bedew'd;
And kissing the bright tribute of thy eye,
Shall after wait like thy good Angel on thee.
There will be none to speak of Ferdinand
Without disdain, if thou diest too: Oh live
A little to defend me, or at least
To say I was no Traitor to thy love,
And lay the shame on death and my false Stars
That would not let me live to be a King.

ROSANIA
Oh Ferdinand,
Thou dost not love me now.

FERDINAND
Not love Rosania?
If wooing thee to live, will not assure thee,

Command me then to die, and spare the cruelty
Of the fair Queen: Not love Rosania?
If thou wilt but delight to see me bleed,
I will at such a narrow passage let
Out life, it shall be many hours in ebbing,
And my soul bathing in the Crimson stream,
Take pleasure to be drown'd. I have small time
To love, and be alive, but I will carry
So true a Faith to woman hence, as shall
Make poor the world, when I am gone to tell
The story yonder.—We are interrupted.

[Enter **KEEPER**.

KEEPER
You must prepare your self for present trial;
I have command to attend you to the Judges.
That Gentleman, and all that did adhere
To your Conspiracy, are by the Queens
Most gracious Mercy pardon'd.

FERDINAND
In that word
Th'hast brought me more then life; I shall betray,
And with my too much joy undo thee again.
Heaven does command thee live, I must obey
This Summons, I shall see thee again Tiberio,
Before I die.

ROSANIA
I'l wait upon you Sir,
The Queen will not deny me that poor office;
I know not how to leave you.

FERDINAND
Death and I
Shall meet, and be made friends; but when we part,
The world shall finde thy story in my heart.

[Exit.

SCENE IV

A Court of Justice.

Enter **OFFICERS** with Bar, Table, Stools,—then **ERNESTO, RODRIGUEZ, LEONARIO, QUEEN**, supported by **LEONARIO, FERDINAND, ROSANIA, LADIES, GENTLEMEN,** and **GUARD**, who set **FERDINAND** to the Bar.

QUEEN
Is that the prisoner at the Bar?

LEONARIO
He that pretended himself Ferdinand,
Your Uncles son.

QUEEN
Proceed to his Arraignment; my Lord Leandro,
You know our pleasure.

LEANDRO
Although the Queen in her own Royal power,
And without violating Sacred Justice, where
Treason comes to invade her, and her Crown
With open war, need not insist upon
The Forms, and Circumstance of Law, but use
Her Sword in present execution;
Yet such is the sweet temper of her blood,
And calmness of her Nature, though provok'd
Into a storm, unto the great'st offender
She shuts up no defence, willing to give
A satisfaction to the world how much
She doth delight in mercy. Ferdinand,
For so thou dost pretend thy self, thou art
Indicted of High Treason to Her Majestie,
In that thou hast usurp'd relation to
Her blood; and under name of being her Kinsman,
Not only hast contriv'd to blast her Honor
With Neighbor Princes, but hast gather'd arms
To wound the precious bosom of her Countrey,
And tear the Crown, which Heaven and just Succession
Hath plac'd upon her Royal Head: what canst
Thou answer to this Treason?

FERDINAND
Boldly thus.
As I was never with the height of all
My expectation, and the aid of Friends,
Transported one degree above my self,
So must not Ferdinand, though his Stars have frown'd
And the great eye of Providence feem to slumber
While your force thus compel'd, & brought me hither
With mockery of my Fate, to be arraign'd
For being a Prince, have any thought beneath

The Title I was born to; yet I'l not call
This cruelty in you, nor in the Queen,
(If I may name her so without injustice
To my own right) a Kingdom is a Garland,
Worth all Contention; and where right seals not
The true Possession, Nature is forgotten,
And blood thought cheap to assure it; there is something
Within that excellent Figure, that restrains
A Passion here, that else would forth like lightning.
Tis not your shape, which yet hath so much sweetness,
Some pale religious Hermit might suspect
You are the blessed Saint he pray'd too; no,
The magick's in our nature, and our blood;
For both our veins full of one precious purple
Strike harmony in their motion, I am Ferdinand,
And you the fair Olivia, brothers children.

LEONARIO
What insolence is this?

QUEEN
Oh my Lord set him
Be free to plead; for if it be no dream,
His cause will want an Orator: By my blood,
He does talk bravely.

RODRIGUEZ
These are flourishes.

ERNESTO
Speak to the treason you are charged with
And confess a guilt.

LEANDRO
He justifies himself.

FERDINAND
If it be treason to be born a Prince,
To have my Fathers Royal Blood move here;
If it be treason, in my infancy
To have escap'd by Divine Providence,
When my poor life should have been sacrific'd
To please a cruel Uncle, whose Ambition
Surpris'd my Crown, and after made Olivia
His Daughter Queen; if it be treason, to
Have been a stranger thus long from my Country,
Bred up with silence, of my name, and birth,
And not till now mature to own my self

Before a Sun-beam; if it be treason
After so long a banishment to weep
A tear of joy upon my Countries bosom,
And call her mine, my just inheritance,
Unless you stain my blood with bastardy;
If it be treason, still to love this Earth,
That knew so many of my race, her Kings,
Though late unkindly arm'd to kill her Sovereign,
As if the effusion of my blood were left
To make her fertile, if to love Olivia,
My nearest pledge of blood, although her power
Hath chain'd her Prince, and made her Lord her prisoner,
Who sits with expectation to hear
That sentence that must make the golden Wreath,
Secure upon her Brow, by blasting mine.
If this be treason, I am guilty Ferdinand.
Your King's become a traitor, and must die
A black, and most inglorious death.

ERNESTO
You offer
At some defence, but come not home; by what
Engine were you translated hence, or whether
Convei'd? There was some trust, deceiv'd, when you
Were carried forth to be preserv'd, and much
Care taken since, in bringing of you up,
And giving secret Fire to this Ambition.

FERDINAND
There wants no testimony here, of what
Concerns the story of my Birth and Infancy,
If one dare speak, and be an honest Lord.

LEANDRO
Hows that?

FERDINAND
Whose love and art secur'd me from all tyranny,
Though here my funeral was believ'd, while I
Sent to an honorable Friend his Kinsman,
Drew safely to the knowledge of my self
At last, till fortune of the War betray'd me
To this captivity.

LEANDRO
I blush at thee
Yong-man, whose fate hath made thee desperate,
And car'st not what mans blood thou draw'st along

In thy black stream, or what mans faith thou mak'st
As hateful as thy crimes.

ERNESTO
That confederate
Sure has some name, declare him, that he may
Thank you for his reward, and lose his head for't.

QUEEN
We always see that men in such high nature
Deform'd and guilty, want not specious shapes
To gain their practice friendship, and compassion,
But he shall feel the punishment; d'you smile?

FERDINAND
A womans anger is but worth it, Madam;
And if I may have freedom, I must say,
Not in contempt of what you seem, nor help'd
By overcharge of passion, which but makes
A fruitless noise; I have a sense of what
I am to lose, a life, but I am so fortified
With valiant thoughts, and innocence, I shall,
When my last breath is giving up to lose
Its self i'th' air, be so remote from fear,
That I will cast my face into one smile,
Which shall when I am dead, acquit all trembling,
And be a story to the world, how free
From paleness Ferdinand took leave of earth.

ROSANIA
Alas my Lord, you forget me, that can
Part with such courage.

FERDINAND
I forget indeed,
I thought of death with honor, but my love
Hath found a way to chide me; O my Boy,
I can weep now.

LEONARIO
A sudden change, he weeps.

QUEEN
What Boy is that?

FERDINAND
I prethee take thy self away.

QUEEN
Your Spirit
Does melt it seems, and you begin to think
A life is worth preserving, though with infamy.

FERDINAND
Goodness thy aid again, and tell this great
Proud woman, I have a Spirit scorns her pity.
Come hither Boy, and let me kiss thee; thus
At parting with a good, and pretty servant,
I can without my honor stain'd shed tears:
I took thee from thy Friends, to make thee mine;
Is it not truth Boy.

ROSANIA
Yes my Lord.

FERDINAND
And mean't when I was King to make thee great,
And shall I not, when I can live no longer,
To cherish thee at farewel, drop a tear?
That I could weep my soul upon thee,—But
You are to slow me thinks, I am so far
From dread, I think your forms too tedious.
I expect my sentence.

QUEEN
Let it stay a while.
What secret flame is this? Honor protect me!
Your Graces fair excuse, for you—I shall
Return again—

[Exit.

FERDINAND
And I, with better guard
After my silence in the Grave, to meet
And plead this cause.

ERNESTO
He is distracted sure;
His person I could pity, but his insolence
Wants an example; what if we proceed
To sentence?

LEONARIO
I suppose the Queen will clear
Your duties in't.

LEANDRO
But I'l acquaint her.

[Exit.

RODRIGUEZ
My Lord Leandro's gone.

ERNESTO
His censure will
Be one with ours.

FERDINAND
Yet shall I publish who
Thou art? I shall not die with a calm soul
And leave thee in this cloud.

[Enter the **QUEEN** and **LEANDRO**.

ROSANIA
By no means Sir.—The Queen.

QUEEN
Whose service is so forward to our State,
That when Our pleasure's known, not to proceed,
They dare be officious in his Sentence? Are
We Queen, or do we move by your Protection?

ERNESTO
Madam, the Prince—

QUEEN
My Lord, you have a Queen.
I not suspect his wisdom Sir, but he
Hath no Commission here to be a Judge,
You were best circumscribe our Regal power,
And by your selves condemn, or pardon all,
And we sign to your will! The offence, which you
Call treason strikes at us, and we release it,
Let me but see one curl in any Brow:
Attend the prisoner hither;

[**FERDINAND** is brought to the state.

—Kiss our hand.
Are you so merciless to think this man
Fit for a Scaffold. You shall Sir be near us,

And if in this confusion of your Fortunes
You can finde gratitude, and love, despair not.
These men that now oppose, may finde your title
Clear to the Kingdom too: Be Sir collected,
And let us use your arm.

[Descends from the state, and exit, supported by **FERDINAND**.

ROSANIA
What change is here!

LEANDRO
What think you of this Lords?

RODRIGUEZ
I dare not think.

LEONARIO
Affronted thus? O my vex'd heart.

[Exit.

ROSANIA
Ile follow still, and if this be no dream,
We have scap'd a Brook, to meet a greater stream.

[Exeunt.

ACT III

SCENE I

The Palace. A Garden.

Enter **RODRIGUEZ, ERNESTO**.

ERNESTO
Though I believ'd her passionate, and like
A Sea, tempestuous in her anger, I
Never thought she would marry him.

RODRIGUEZ
She's the Queen.
But with what honor she could quit the Prince,
Who (without treason) did deserve her too,
Comes not within my reach.

ERNESTO
If you consider
He has been valiant for her to great purpose,
And brought a prisoner home, to mount his Gennet:
It was a pretty service.

RODRIGUEZ
How does he bear it.

ERNESTO
He's here you may enquire it.

[Enter **LEONARIO** with Letters and a **SERVANT**.

LEONARIO
Be swift and faithful, Arragon bleeds here,
Nothing but War can right my cause and honor.

SERVANT
Expect an army great as your own thoughts
To cut the way to your revenge.

[Exit.

LEONARIO
My Lords Rodriguez and Ernesto.

RODRIGUEZ and **ERNESTO**
Your Graces servants.

LEONARIO
A man may take the benefit of this Garden,
Without a Court offence, you have had the day
Of triumph, and the Queen already teeming,
To bless the Kingdom with an Heir; and yet
You see I walk like a poor Neighbor Prince,
And have my heart still.

RODRIGUEZ
I am glad you bear it so.

LEONARIO
Not have I a meaning
To run my self into despair, or strangle
My better hopes, out of pure melancholy.
I praise the influence of my Stars; there is
A fire in Cupids Quiver, that will scorch

Through armor; and what's womans flesh and blood
To make resistance, though I did not dance
Upon the marriage night, I wish'd her joyes
I' th' morning.

ERNESTO
Her heart shew'd she was pleas'd
With what she had done; she was as active as
The air before she went to Bed.

RODRIGUEZ
But I
Observ'd a declination in the King,
And as the night approach'd which should have more
Inlarg'd his mirth, he grew more melancholy.

LEONARIO
Strange! And such a Bride that took him from
So great a loss, to place him in her bosom;
But he was mark'd for the Queens thoughts, and I
By destiny to bring this pair of Pidgeons
Together. I expect no more reward,
The Willow Garland Crowns me, but the Prince
Is here still.

ERNESTO
Your highness hath a noble temper.

RODRIGUEZ
How ere he seem to cover it, his soul
Hath a deep apprehension of the affront.
Let's leave him, our discourse may be displeasing.
We are servants to your Grace.

[Exeunt **RODRIGUEZ** and **ERNESTO**.

LEONARIO
Y'have honor'd me.
Think I am tame still? let the inconstant Queen
Secure her thoughts, and glory in my silence;
This heart is laboring a revenge.

[Enter **CAPTAIN**.

Captain, what news? the Court is merry still?

CAPTAIN
Not altogether so merry as it was hop'd for.

LEONARIO
Can there be an eclipse already?

CAPTAIN
I have not read the Almanack for this year,
But by my Court Astronomie, I finde
Our Sun and Moon are in no Conjunction;
They take their fit by turns, the King was cold
And full of flegm last night, and they that wait
Near both, report the Queen this morning look'd
As she had wept.

LEONARIO
O, tears of joy.

CAPTAIN
Of anger rather, if you saw her fullenness.
She frowns on every man, she turn'd away
One of her servants but this morning for
Presenting her with Verses, that did praise
The King, and wish her fruitful. Her own Page
Was whipt for saying the King lay with the Queen
And might for ought he knew▪ get her with childe ere morning.

LEONARIO
Thou art humorous.

CAPTAIN
And so are they.

LEONARIO
This begins well; and what
Do people talk abroad of me, and my
Affront?

CAPTAIN
Why, they say they are sorry for you,
Especially the women.

LEONARIO
Thou art pleasant.

CAPTAIN
Some that are cheif in counsel, privately
Suspect it but a trick of State; and that
You had discover'd underhand the Queen
Was not—

LEONARIO
Leave this mirth; let me indear thy care
For my intelligence at Court;

[Gives him money.

I must
Not off so tamely; and expect me here,
After a small dispatch, I have more to impart.

[Exit.

CAPTAIN
Your humble creature still Sir. 'Las poor Gent'
Were has capable to be entertain'd now, in revenge
I would mount all the Madams in the Court,
There should be nothing like a woman in't,
But I would touz and tumble: Who are these?

[Enter **3RD** and **4TH CITIZENS**.

3RD CITIZEN
Save you Sir.

CAPTAIN
It may be so.

4TH CITIZEN
Pray Sir take no offence, we have been enquiring
About the Court for two Gentlemen.

CAPTAIN
And cannot your four eies see two Gentlemen
I' th' Court?

3RD CITIZEN
Excuse us Sir, we have seen many, you
May guess we have relation to the Citie Sir,
And would be glad to meet two of our old acquaintances,
A brace of our Tribe,
We hear, translated first out of the Citie,
To be Sons o'th' Sword, are since turn'd Courtiers.
Pray d'ye know 'em?

[Enter **1ST CITIZEN** dressed like a Courtier and **VIOLINDA**.

CAPTAIN

Yes children of the Gown, but their imployment
Will not give 'em leave to attend such vulgar conference,
And here comes one of the Moon-calves, does he look
Like a Haberdasher, that's one of the Maids of Honor,
The Weisel loves a Hens-Nest, and I have setled
This perswasion, That no woman can hold out,
Now he is sworn a servant extraordinary.

3RD CITIZEN
Sir do you know us?

1ST CITIZEN
No.

4TH CITIZEN
We were your neighbors, and of the same trade.

CAPTAIN
They'l make him sweat; how the Rogue glotes upon 'em.

3RD CITIZEN
We were of your acquaintance, when you sold Garters.

1ST CITIZEN
Go hang your selves.

4TH CITIZEN
And Statute-lace.

VIOLINDA
What are these?

1ST CITIZEN
Poor men, that had some losses late by fire,
And would become my Clients to procure
Some Letters Patents to beg by; alas, they are half distracted.

3RD CITIZEN
He's proud—I have a parcel of Periwigs
Please you, sir, for old acquaintance, put 'em off for me,
Among some friends of yours at Court, whose skulls
Are but thinly furnish'd; the hair is of a
Gentlewomans spinning.

CAPTAIN
I could love this Citizen, and ow him any money
For his confident abusing him.

[Exit **VIOLINDA**.

He has brib'd her absence with some Ring or Bracelet,
Least she should taste the discovery now.

3RD CITIZEN
Methinks you need not be so proud.

1ST CITIZEN
I would have you to know that I am an extraordinary—

CAPTAIN
Proud Coxcomb.

1ST CITIZEN
Servant to the Queen. What I was,
I am willing to forget;
What you are, is apparant, I defie the
Dunghil I came from, and it is scandalum
Magnatum to be so saucy.

[Exit.

3RD CITIZEN
I will not leave your worship so.

[Exit.

CAPTAIN
What will this Rascal do with himself?
Here comes the other Fool to make up the Gemini.

[Enter **2ND CITIZEN**, dressed like a Courtier with two Petitions.

2ND CITIZEN
Hum, I will not know him—Let me see—
The humble Petition of—

4TH CITIZEN
Save you Master—

2ND CITIZEN
Prethee fellow do not trouble me—
Humbly praying—The Queen shall sign it.
Let me see this other—

CAPTAIN
Who the devil will bring him a Petition,

This Whelp has discovered him, and now would
Pretend himself most busily employ'd
About Petitions to the Queen.

2ND CITIZEN
Hum, shall daily pray for—Hum.

CAPTAIN
More wit and money a your side; for your
Extraordinary place will not hold out.

4TH CITIZEN
Sir I have a sute to you.

2ND CITIZEN
Is it Embroidered Sattin Sir, or Scarlet?
Yet if your business do hold weight and consequence,
I may deserve to wear your thankfulness
In Tissue or cloth of Bodkin; Ermines are for Princes.

4TH CITIZEN
Alas my Suite is not worth your wearing.

2ND CITIZEN
Good faith Sir you must excuse me, at this time
My attendance is expected at the Counsel, come
To my Chamber by five a clock in the morning
Four days hence, and you shall be sure to finde
Me—

CAPTAIN
Asleep.

4TH CITIZEN
But do you not know me?

2ND CITIZEN
Hum! Yes I have seen your phisnomy, were you
Never in a conspicuous place, called the Pillorie.

4TH CITIZEN
How! the Pillory?

CAPTAIN
A skirmish, and it be thy will!

4TH CITIZEN
If it were not in the Court Garden,

I would beat out thy brains.

2ND CITIZEN
Take heed, for I am an extraordinary—

4TH CITIZEN
Rat-catcher.

CAPTAIN
You may beat out his brains here as securely Sir,
As if you met him i'th' market; Marry if you do
Not kill him outright, it is but the loss
Of your hand.

4TH CITIZEN
I would it were but the loss of my left hand
To beat one of thy eyes out—Are you an Ancient?

2ND CITIZEN
Thank you for that, so I might deserve
To be beaten. I am an extraordinary Sir.

CAPTAIN
And deserves to be beaten accordingly.
You may kick him without danger.

4TH CITIZEN
May I?

[Enter **3RD CITIZEN** kicking the **1ST CITIZEN**.

CAPTAIN
Look, your friend will shew you a president'
He is acquainted with the Court latitude.

3RD CITIZEN
This is no striking.

1ST CITIZEN
I know it is not.

CAPTAIN
They are subtle knaves, and know the Law.

1ST CITIZEN
A pox upon 'em, I feel it.

2ND CITIZEN

At their peril say I, these poor things
Do not believe that we are extraordinary men,
I shall know you another time, I shall.

CAPTAIN
If you had known him now it had been better
For your haunches. Well, I ha' not done with
These whelps yet, till they are undone.
I shall never be sufficiently revenged for their affront
At Court. The Prince commanded me to
Expect his return here, I'll not leave
The Garden.

[Enter **ROSANIA**.

Who's this?

[Retires behind shrubbery.

ROSANIA
Is perjury no sin? or can Heaven be
So busie or a sleep? Such crimes of men
Pass with impunity? Let this wake your anger:
This; Ferdinand is married, all his vows
Scatter'd in th' air, dispers'd like wither'd leaves,
And hurried on the wings of some rude Wind,
Whose pride was to deflower the Spring; Oh Ferdinand,
Couldst thou, whilst yet thy breath was warm with love,
With love of me, call back thy faith, and tear
Thy Heart from mine to plant it in her Bosom?

CAPTAIN
How's this?

ROSANIA
What though she be a Queen? could any thirst
Of present title flatter thy Soul from me?
I that left all for thee, and would have call'd
Death for thy cause a triumph, now must live
The scorn of my own thoughts, despis'd by thee.

CAPTAIN
Here's a new business; this obscures me quaintly.

[Enter **LEANDRO**.

LEANDRO
The King commands you not to leave the Garden.

He espied you from the Gallerie Window, and
Would have you here attend him.

ROSANIA
Sir, may I
Without offence, ask if the King be merry?

LEANDRO
We are scarce yet acquainted with his nature,
But we observe no Jubilie in his eyes,
Nor is the Queen so pleasant as our hopes
Did promise after Marriage.

ROSANIA
Pray excuse this boldness.

LEANDRO
You'l expect his pleasure here?

[Exit.

ROSANIA
'Tis my ambition once more to see,
And speak with him, and if his language break not
My Heart, I'll take my leave—the Queen.

[Retires.

[Enter **QUEEN**, **LEANDRO**.

LEANDRO
He is a Servant to whom the King
Was pleas'd to shew affection, when he had
No expectation of your Royall favour.

QUEEN
I do remember, I observ'd him once
Use more than common passion to this servant,
And if we may build any confidence
Upon a fair aspect, he may deserve it.
Say we would speak with him; my Heart's opprest
With melancholy, something tels my spirit
I am too tame; have I advanc'd a thing
Without a name to perch on the same Cloud
With me and for his sake slighted a Prince,
My Honour, and his Faith transported with
My folly and his charms of tongue and person?
And dares he pay me with neglect and coldness?

Oh my vext soul! but he shall find I have
A sense of my dishonour; and yet open
Wayes become trivial and poor revengers,
I will doe something that shall sting him to
Repentance;

[**LEANDRO** brings forward **ROSANIA**.

My Lord you now may leave us.

[Exit **LEANDRO**.

Sir of what Country are you?

ROSANIA
Of Valencia.

QUEEN
Your name?

ROSANIA
Tiberio.
My Parents not ignoble, yet too hasty
I'th' apprehension of Prince Ferdinand;
His Fortune (if I may yet call him so)
Gave me to be his page I must confess
My diligence thriv'd so well since I came to him,
That he did value me above his servant.

QUEEN
Yet I've not seen you wait since we were married.

ROSANIA
It was no want of dutie Madam, I
Had late some wrestling with a Fever that
Compel'd me to my Chamber, and disabled me
For fit attendance.

QUEEN
Why dost weep?

ROSANIA
I Madam?

QUEEN
I see the tears.

ROSANIA

They are not sorrow then to see my Master
Possest of so much happiness in your love,
And I am confident his soul so full
Of Honour and regard to your great virtues
Will seal him worth your gracious favours Madam,
And the worlds Envie.

QUEEN
I'll not blame him now
For loving thee; and so much hath thy faith
And innocence prevail'd, thou sha't translate
Thy service, and be mine, he shall consent.

ROSANIA
I am to both most humble.

QUEEN
Prethee tell me,
Making so much of thee, he do's impart
Sometimes the secrets of his bosom to thee.
Tell me what fault he has, for thou know'st all.

ROSANIA
'Las Madam I know none,
Or if I did, it ill became the trust
And dutie of a servant to reveal'em

QUEEN
Thou wer't his bed-fellow?

ROSANIA
Gracious Madam—

QUEEN
Do's he not wanton in the night, and talk
Of Mistresses.

ROSANIA
By truth not to me, Madam.

QUEEN
Dissemble not
I know he has a Mistress.

ROSANIA
If love were ever so unkind to him—

QUEEN

Unkind? why I'st a sin to love? I shall
Suspect thy Youth has not been free, thy looks
Betray some seeds of Love.

ROSANIA
By all that's good
I never was in love but with my Master.

CAPTAIN
Good.

QUEEN
He is not worth it.

ROSANIA
Madam.

QUEEN
Be wise, and govern well thy hopes. I'll help
Thee to a Mistress; th'ast no Mistress yet?

ROSANIA
But you self Madam.

QUEEN
It shall be no other.
Thy Master is ingrateful

ROSANIA
Goodness aid him.

QUEEN
And wisdom thee, thou art a pretty youth,
I will reward thee better, if thou canst
Be faithfull and obey.

ROSANIA
In all things Madam
That shall become your creature.

QUEEN
'Tis not safe
To play with a Queens favours, you shall want
Neer us, forget thy Master, and be happy.

[Exit.

ROSANIA

What clue can guide me in this Labyrinth?
I would when I had lost Ferdinands Heart
I had lost my understanding! She returns.

[Enter **QUEEN**.

QUEEN
The King is coming this way; now be free,
Thou sha't have reason afterwards to bless
Thy fate, this cannot chose but vex him.

[The **QUEEN** is pleasant with **ROSANIA**.

[Enter **FERDINAND**.

FERDINAND
The Queen so pleasant? she has lost her sullenness,
Playes with his Hair, and smiles.

ROSANIA
Madam, the King
Observes us.

FERDINAND
Strokes his cheek too, she does want
A Ganimede; my poor Rosania
Art thou the path she walks on to revenge,
All is not well within her Heart; but mine
Sinks with the heavy pressure.

[Exit **QUEEN**.

—she is gone.
The Queen does grace you much Tiberio,
Those favours are not common.

ROSANIA
She is pleas'd
For your sake Sir to cast some smile upon me.
I know 'twas your request she should be kind,
To keep my Heart a live.

FERDINAND
Th'art not discover'd.

ROSANIA
Did not you discourse
My story to her?

FERDINAND
I?

ROSANIA
Take heed, yet this
Will adde but a thin Feather to the scale
Of my misfortune, she knows all, and, in
The pittie of my sufferings sayes you are
Not worth my love, and calls you most ingrateful

FERDINAND
We are both lost, till now there was some hope
How to repair thy sorrow.

ROSANIA
Do not mock me;
'Tis a worse tyranny than to kill, to laugh
At what you have made wretched, 'tis as possible
To call past ages back.

FERDINAND
Take heed Rosania,
And be not Judge of what thou know'st not, dearest.

ROSANIA
I know too much.

FERDINAND
That I am Married.

ROSANIA
Ther's no truth in Man.

FERDINAND
You are too rash; for there is truth in me,
In Ferdinand, though in thy thoughts held black
And staind prodigiously with breach of faith,
I have not broke my vow, do not compell me
By thy unbelief to do a Sin I hate
As much as I love thee.

ROSANIA
Have you a Soul?

FERDINAND
Yes, and thy Eye shall read it, be but calm,
That Soul, thou once didst love, white with his first

Simplicity and faith; I wo'not urge
In my excuse the beautie of the Queen
Enough to melt a Scythian into love,
But call to mind my dear Rosania,
And do but put upon thee Ferdinand
So late forgotten by his Stars, a prisoner,
Slav'd like a villain at the bar, expecting
At every breath his sentence, nay admit
Rosania, the best part of his Soul
Stood like a weeping fountain to take leave
Of what she never must salute agen:
In this extreme, to preserve Ferdinand
And save Rosania, wouldst thou scorn the breath
Of mercy, that did Court thee from the Lips
Of a great Queen? couldst thou love Rosania,
If thou wert Ferdinand to lose thy self?
Whom she would follow in a stream of tears,
And when she had made an island of thy tomb,
Striving to swim to thee, she could not choose,
But drown her self in her own waves. I prethee
Take reason to thee, and when th'ast consider'd—

ROSANIA
Perswade me I am not Rosania,
And I will say 'tis virtue and that yet
Your heart may grow with mine; is not the Queen
Possest of that which should have been my title,
A Wife to Ferdinand?

FERDINAND
'Tis confest the world
Doth think it so, I did consent to ceremony.

ROSANIA
Call you injoying of the Queen but ceremony?

FERDINAND
Pause there, and if thou hast but so much charity
To think I dare not blaspheme Heaven, I'l call
That, and the Angels boldly to my witness,
The Queen's to me a stranger yet.

ROSANIA
A miracle.

FERDINAND
Retain but love, as thou preserv'st thy sweetness,
And that will teach thee to believe that Ferdinand,

How ere saluted King is still thy subject,
And though her Husband, in my faith to thee
The Marriage-Bed hath still our Virgin sheets;
A Brother might embrace a Sister, with
The heat I brought; that this is truth, the power
And name I have, shall only serve to make
Our flight secure into another Kingdom,
And when I part with these new shining glories.
Thy faith will be confirm'd, and thou acknowledge
I ventur'd much to keep my Heart thy servant.

ROSANIA
I know not what to say; is not the Queen
Displeas'd?

FERDINAND
She is, but cunningly disguiseth
Her passion to the World; but I forgot
What must inlarge my fears of her revenge
If thou be known Rosania.

ROSANIA
Lose that fear,
I am still safe, and now I see the cause
Makes her repent her favours, and thy greatness;
Forgive me Ferdinand; and yet I know not,
All is not well ther's poyson in this Balsam
Prepar'd for thee.

FERDINAND
From whom?

ROSANIA
Rosania.

FERDINAND
When she shall but consent to have me dye,
She shall not trouble poyson to send off
My despis'd life, my soul in just obedience
To her command will take a cheerful flight
In hope to serve her in the other World.

ROSANIA
You shall know more hereafter, and let this
Secure your thoughts, she yet believes me what
This shape presents, but without wise prevention,
I fear I shall not live too long conceal'd;
I dare not say her honour is a bleeding,

But a Queen thus distasted may not find
That Ice within her blood; we are interrupted.

[Enter **RODRIGUEZ**.

RODRIGUEZ
Your pardon Sir; 'tis the Queens pleasure
This Gentleman attend her in the Gallery.

FERDINAND
He shall wait her commands—

[Exit **RODRIGUEZ**

I know not what to counsell, 'tis not safe
Sweet to neglect her, yet my fears of some
Ill fate, are round about me like a mist,
And dark my understandings; let a kiss
And silence teach our souls some new discourse.

CAPTAIN
Why here's a volume of Intelligence.
I'll stay no longer to expect the Prince,
But seek him out immediatly; disguises?
King by your leave, I shall untruss your Mistress.

[Exit

ROSANIA
I know not what I feel, nor what to fear,
If love e'r meant a Tragedie; 'tis here.

FERDINAND
If we ne'r meet agen, one more salute
Shall fortifie our lives by joyning breath,
Nor shall our last hard fate deny us this,
To change our faithfull Souls at our last kiss.

[Exeunt severally.

ACT IV

SCENE I

An Apartment in the Palace.

Enter **RODRIGUEZ, LEANDRO, ERNESTO**.

ERNESTO
I know not what to think on't, but if I
Have any sense, there is some new state madness
Crept into Court.

RODRIGUEZ
Are we not all a sleep,
And these fine dreams perplex us?

LEANDRO
No 'tis waking.

RODRIGUEZ.
Shew me the renth part of a reason why
The Queen did Marry him.

LEANDRO
'Twas destinie.

ERNESTO
Why since should he be melancholy?

RODRIGUEZ
Or she so humorus?

ERNESTO
Not lie together? pray Heaven the Gentleman
Be found with no defective title in him.

LEANDRO
Observe her favours to that Boy, he was
His servant, now her minion. I like not
These violent wheels; the whole frame may be soon
Indanger'd, if these passions be not cur'd.

RODRIGUEZ
New lodgings for him, neer her own, and he
Given free access to the Bed chamber.

LEANDRO
'Tis naught
Or will be so, I pittie the good King;
Though she have rais'd him to the highest glorie
Her power extended too, yet to make this height
His precipice, and throw him into scorn,
Nay poyson the best hopes he had of honour,

And love from her, and in his sight to Court
A Boy, his servant? It would vex the best
Of all our tempers, if we felt the sting on't.

[Enter **ROSANIA** and **VIOLINDA** pass over the Stage.

ERNESTO
He's here, that Lady is the Queens Cabinet.

LEANDRO
They are merry about the Mouth.

ERNESTO
Another summons?
'Tis possible the Queen may Marry him too.

LEANDRO
There is some mysterie we cannot reach.
If we doe well remember, ther's a Law
Made by her self, as soon as she was Queen,
To keep Wifes Pulses temperat, and correct
The insolent Blood of Women that had Husbands.

ERNESTO
And Men were not exempted.

LEANDRO
I say no more.
But Heaven maintain the Law, and the Law-makers,
And conjure down that Devill,
'Tis the King and the smooth Boy, lets leave 'em.

[Exeunt **LORDS**.

[Enter **FERDINAND**, and **ROSANIA**.

FERDINAND
Was this the Ladies Message? does the Queen
Take thee into such favour?

ROSANIA
I tell truth,
And though it found but ill on the Queens part,
Because she thinks me what I seem my Lord,
You need not to wear one Cloud upon your Face
When you remember who I am, my fears
Are thick upon my Heart, how to secure
This shadow any longer.

FERDINAND
That afflicts
Me most Rosania, for it pleases me
To hear she can affect thee; but what way
To keep her expectation high, and thee
(My dearest) safe? her passions may be violent.

ROSANIA
They are already Sir, if I mistake not;
I wish to Heaven that you were reconcil'd
To do the office of a Husband to her;
That peace would keep her Bosom clear, and I
Should live to all the World except your self
A stranger still.

FERDINAND
What language speaks Rosania?
There's death in every syllable. Should I
Obey what thou desir'st, and do the office
Of a Husband, Ha!

ROSANIA
I'll wait upon you still,
And hope you will vouchsafe me now and then
A harmless smile; her beauty will deserve
Your whole heart, and there's something in the memory
Of what she has advanc'd you to, will help
To make you kind.

FERDINAND
Should I injoy the Queen?
Because the misery of my fate compeld
A ceremonious sin? shall I betray
The essence of my faith, and leave a curse,
When thou art known, upon my name for ever?
If thou hast taken new resolves against me,
Punish my heart some other way; had she
More ornament than ever met in woman,
Mistress of more perfection than Poets
Invented for the Queen of love to this
Were the proud Empire of the World her own,
And she would make me Lord of her, and these,
It would not buy me to the pleasure of
One Nights embrace, my body shall not carry
My soul so far astray; the Man condemn'd
To live in a perpetual Snow, hath not
A purer Frost within his blood.

ROSANIA
This but
Engenders a new grief, although it bind
Rosanias Heart there is yet one way left
And that ere I pronounce you must forgive;
There is a trembling in my tongue and I
Already feel such Winter in my breath,
My timorous Lips do wither.

FERDINAND
Do not fright
My Soul too much, ther's something threatens me
So like a loss of these, that I am left
A piece of shaking Earth death cannot look
To make me tremble so; canst thou forsake me?

ROSANIA
Not in my Heart, but give my body leave
To seek some other place my Lord to dwell in.
When I am gone into some wilderness,
You will find ease at Heart, and love the Queen,
And perfect all; I'll pray you may live happy,
And hold Intelligence with some gentle Winds
That shall convey my wishes and return
What joys do follow you; the purling Rivers
I'll teach your name and they which guide this way
Shall bring thee something Ferdinand of mine;
My tears I know will not be lost, which I
Will send thee daily by the courteous stream,
Clear pledges of my faith; consent my Lord
I may depart and you shall choose your way,
To every blessing here.

FERDINAND
Not till we meet
With one embrace, and take our flight together;
And I have thought a way to perfect it,
Observe my sweet Rosania, the Queen
Thou sayst affects thee, cherish it, with all
The softness of her creature; if she allow,
Kiss her, and promise what young lovers doe,
Examine not, but by thy love to me
Be free in amorous language, if she have
Heat to a private meeting in her Chamber,
Obey, this shall secure our loves ambition.
Enquire not, but resolve, and let me know
The time.

ROSANIA
You will attempt no violence
Upon the Queen?

FERDINAND
By this—

[Kisses her.

ROSANIA
What if she have commanded me
This Night?

FERDINAND
To meet?

ROSANIA
In her Bed-Chamber.

FERDINAND
Ha! Obey it.

ROSANIA
At a late hour.

FERDINAND
It shall beget our comfort
If thou consent.

ROSANIA
But shall I not expose
My self to danger, if her love persue
Immodest ends, since you advise I should
Apply my self to her desires?

FERDINAND
If she
Take too much flame, by some soft art delay her,
Till I come to close all; keep still thy person
Secret, the least discovery will destroy
Us both; the Evening with much hast prepares
Thy visit and our happiness.

ROSANIA
I'l obey,
But be you sure to come.

FERDINAND
Lose thou no time
Now to indear thee to her, let us part
Love will find balm to cure the wounded Heart.

[Exeunt severally

SCENE II

The Palace. The Queen's Apartment.

A Table, and Lights, set out, then enter **QUEEN**, and **VIOLINDA**.

QUEEN
Was he not cheerful when he promis'd thee?

VIOLINDA
He was, and he was not.

QUEEN
I have a strange apprehension, and this doth feed it.

VIOLINDA
I told him 'twas an honour worth his joyful entertainment.

QUEEN
If it should prove succesful, my revenge
Were perfect, I'm resolute to persue—

VIOLINDA
It makes well
For your contrivement that the King and you do
Lodge at distance—stay, I hear a tread.

QUEEN
I hope 'tis he.

[Enter **LEONARIO**.

VIOLINDA
Prince Leonario Madam.

QUEEN
What comes he for?

LEONARIO

Although I have small expectation
For my own sake, that you can pardon Madam
This bold access, and at so dark an hour,
Yet when you have heard my business, You will know
Your self so much concern'd, I'l not despair
To find your mercy.

QUEEN
You prepare me for
Something of consequence.

LEONARIO
Please you to dismiss
Your Ladie, I have something to deliver
Wil' not become her knowledge.

QUEEN
Leave us—

[Exit **VIOLINDA**.

Now
Our conference is free, your Graces pleasure?
It must be matter of much essence, that
Could not expect till morning, but y'ar welcome.

LEONARIO
This time and darkness Madam best becomes him,
Who for your sake blushes to see the Day,
But I came not to chide my wrongs have learn'd
A modest silence, my approach is not
To name a suffering of mine, but to
Discover what already is prepar'd
Against your peace and honour.

QUEEN
Is it treason?

LEONARIO
It is, but threatens not your life, you may
Live many years upon the wound.

QUEEN
You fright me.

LEONARIO
Lose not the beauty of your cheek so soon,
Hide not beneath that cold and killing Snow,

One Rosie blush; and yet that pale would shew
Like Innocence which you have lost; oh Madam
Had you not made a forfet of your truth
To me, no storm could shake you, but your soul
That made no change, could know no fear; I come
To tell you what just providence hath done
In my revenge, your breach of vow is punish'd
With loss of faith in him, to whom you gave
The Heart you promis'd me, the King, whose pride
You built on my dishonour, is as false,
As you were.

QUEEN
This is passion but be
Not yet too rash in censuring him. Whom I
Have plac'd so near, I must defend, nor will
He need my strength, to make their blood account
That dare traduce his honour; he has a Heart—

LEONARIO
A false one. I was born without a fear,
And dare upon his bosom (wear he worth
The manly contestation) write him perjur'd.

QUEEN
I would this were not envy; but admit
He be thus guiltie, 'tis a fault in him.

LEONARIO
No Madam, it is yours; that sin that poysond
The expectation of my joys in you.
Hath made him false and will excuse his storie,
When you are nam'd that broke your faith to me;
I can have no hope now to be repair'd,
But if it be worth memorie to know
The triumph waits on Innocence, the World
Shall say the Queen deserv'd to meet a scorn
Deep as her wrongs to me.

QUEEN
It cannot be.

LEONARIO
Think so, and help to make the revenge greater,
Till the winds catch the black report, and multiply
The shame, by scattering it about the Kingdom,
Sit still, and careless of your fame, incourage
His private lust, his Mistress now in Court.

QUEEN
A Mistriss in the Court?

LEONARIO
Yes Madam, in the Court,
And may one day think any second place
Too narrow to contain her greatness; she—

QUEEN
As y'ar a Prince no more; I have done ill,
And find the penance here, It does agree
With his neglects, and addes new flame to my
Young jealousie; I feel a tempest rising;
By all your goodness leave me Sir; I cannot
Now right you more than mourn, and give belief to you.
No more I pray you, by all your love to honour.

LEONARIO
I ha' done,
And take my leave, my everlasting leave,
'Tis time; how like the day, that flatter'd us
With cheerful light, are my desires fled hence,
And left me here a prodigie of darkness,
A walking Herse, hung round about with night,
Whose wings must one day cover all? farewell.
If any Star look forth, it is to call
Me hence, and light me to another World.
Our Lips are never like to meet agen.

[Kisses

Farewell, if I but stay, I shall forgive her.

[Exit.

QUEEN
A Mistress in the Court? something is busie
About my Heart.

[Enter **VIOLINDA**.

VIOLINDA
The Prince is gone.

QUEEN
No matter.

[Exit **VIOLINDA**

Affronted thus? but I forgot to ask
Her name that rivals me; how this passion
Befools our understanding, and prevents
The knowledge, and the cure of what afflicts us!
The Morning will assure all, but shall this
Strike me to ashes? I may find a way
To my revenge.

[Enter **VIOLINDA**.

VIOLINDA
Tiberio is come Madam.

QUEEN
Wait carefully.

VIOLINDA
I know my dutie.

[Exit.

[Enter **ROSANIA**: Kneels and Kisses her Hand.

QUEEN
Rise,
This meeting was not meant for ceremony,
Ther's something in this presence will deserve
We should put off all state, and speak like friends.
You must be cover'd too. I'll have it so.
We are private now.

ROSANIA
These graces will
Undoe a youth, whose birth, and careless Stars
Ordain'd him to be humble, and with dutie
Wait on your meanest servant.

QUEEN
Thou shalt soon have cause
To think thy Stars are careful of thee, if
Thou canst be wise.

ROSANIA
Alas! my years are few.

QUEEN

Thy knowledge is not wanting to distinguish
Whose favours Court thee, and apply thy self
To understand, and thank the kind bestower;
'Tis in my power to make thee great.

ROSANIA
You may
Advance this worthless walking shadow Madam,
And when you like the free and bounteous Sun
Have blest me with your rayes, it is but like
His glorious warmth bestow'd upon a peece
Of rude and barren Earth, which takes not from
The lustre of your Beams, but shews more clearly,
By your own light, what poverty you shin'd on.

QUEEN
This modesty becomes you not, look in
My eye, and read what's there.

ROSANIA
Some thing like anger,
Enough to strike me dead.

QUEEN
What now?

ROSANIA
A smile,
And such attending sweetness—

QUEEN
Thus it shall
Invite thee still to gaze, and love, Tiberio,
No frown shall point on thee; I finde my eyes
Were meant for thee, and all they grac'd before,
But objects of mistake. Here here, O turn
Thy lovely face away, lest I be seen
To blush, my heart hath chose to place my love
And the reward; this would become thy tongue
A great deal better, Come sit down Tiberio.
What still an Infants understanding? Think
I am the man, and learn a little better,
What beauty dwells upon this hand, What softness,
How like the Snow, or Innocence it shews,
Yet fires my heart with every gentle touch.

ROSANIA [aside]
Dear Madam; would the King would come.

QUEEN
This is a happiness that Kings should sue for,
And yet there are poor comforts in these Kisses;
Let hands preserve Societie with hands,
And with their change of whiteness, and of Balm,
Make wealthy one another: But let what
Was mean't for kisses meet, and finde out pleasure
By warm exchange of souls from our soft lips.

[Kisses.

Madam, how like you this?

ROSANIA
Madam.

QUEEN
I suppose you a Lady all this while,
And I the man, our lips must meet again,
Will this instruct thee nothing?

[Kisses.

ROSANIA
Gracious Madam.

QUEEN
And yet this recreation comes short,
Dear Lady, of what love might well allow us.
Admit you are a Queen, you are not bound
To thin your Royal Blood with frost, but as
Your power, your pleasure should exceed; nay grant
You have a man (a man said I) that can
Keep love alive, and warm a yielding bosom,
Yet where from the invitement of your eye,
And amorous choice, I am become your servant,
You may be a little kinder.

ROSANIA
Madam, I know not
How with the safetie of my self, my dutie,
And your own name and power, to understand you,
(Yet this to some would need but little Comment)
Can you place such a value on a thing
That not deserves to breath your name? Or should
I hope these charms of Language you have spred
To catch my heart, which hath no wings, but where

It can believe; For you transcend so much
In wonder of your love, a willing Faith
Not easily can reach it. But dear Madam,
I know all this is but to try my duty,
And you have pleas'd to choose me forth, to make
These silent hours more grateful, by the mirth
My weak replies may raise you,

QUEEN
Miracle!
I but imagin'd thee a woman, now
I shall believe thee one indeed; this coldness
Becomes no masculine habit. Come, we'll in,
And change our Sexes; Thou shalt wear my clothes,
And I will put on these, help on with thine,
And I will dress thee handsomely, and then
We'll act again.

ROSANIA [aside]
Not for the world dear Madam. Not yet come?

QUEEN
The world? This confirms my jealousie.
I'll search you to the soul, Adonis come,
I'll call thee so, and court thee with more charm
Than Venus did, when in the Idalian Groves
To buy a kiss, she offer'd the proud Boy
Her flaming Chariot, and her Doves of Snow.
'Tis in thy power to make thy fate and heart
More happy by consent to meet with mine;
Tempt not the anger of a Queen despis'd,
Whose breath can like a whirl-wind snatch thee up,
And drop thee in a Wilderness, where with sorrow
For thy neglect, thou by degrees maist sigh
Thy self into a Mist, which no Sun-beam
Shall pitie or take up into a Cloud.
But love me, and compose thy heart to mine,
Wee'l live with more delight, than fancie can
Inrich Elizium with. The soft hours shall stay
Till we allow 'em Wings, and while we kiss
And on each others Lips breath Incense thus,

[Kisses her.

Wee'l have ten thousand Capids for our guard,
Whose Bows shall awe the destinies, and we write
The King and Queen of Fate.

[Enter **FERDINAND, LEANDRO, RODRIGUEZ, ERNESTO, CAPTAIN, GUARD.**

FERDINAND
Will this deserve your faith?

LEANDRO
We must believe.

[Enter **VIOLINDA.**

VIOLINDA
We are undone, the King.

QUEEN
False Keys?

ROSANIA
'Twas time to come.

FERDINAND
Had I not cause, my Lords, to appear sad,
When I suspected this so great affront?
My melancholy all this while was but
A mourning for this shame: Look but my Lords
Into yourselves, and make this suffering yours.

VIOLINDA
Madam be rais'd again, I have an art
To fetch you off with honor, and the youth too.
I will persuade him there can be no cure
In this extreme but to pretend himself
A woman; I will dress him in your Gown
Before they can be ware on't; they all know
This way he cannot flie, mean time put on
A confidence, and let them know you are
The Queen, not to be shaken with their power;
This will gain time.

QUEEN
Prosper in this.

VIOLINDA
I will
Redeem my fault, or never sleep again.

[Exit with **ROSANIA.**

FERDINAND

She blushes not.
Were she not Queen, what names could we bestow
Upon this want of modesty?

LEANDRO
'Tis plain.
We came in time.

FERDINAND
Most happily to prevent
Some further act of shame;
Can she look on us
Without a blush?

QUEEN
I see no such attraction
In your state faces that I should desire
Much to look on 'em. Who made you King I pray?

FERDINAND
Your power I dare not call it love, presuming
That I was fit to be your property,
Without a soul to see, or have a sense
Of these dishonors; This rank heap of blood,
Madam, what penitence can make this clear?
Admit your thoughts were wanton, and your flame,
Too great to be supprest, could you finde none
For your adulterate embrace, but one
That was my servant? my own hound devour me?
As if your lust had not enough of shame
And mischief to me, but your malice must
Appear in't too; with what securitie
Can I expect to live, when she begins
So soon to poyson me?

LEANDRO
We heard her say
They two would write themselves the King and Queen.

RODRIGUEZ
So we did all.

FERDINAND
You may consider these.

LEANDRO
'Tis impious
Madam with what grief do we

Remember now that Law you made
After your Corronation to preserve
The name of your sex chast which gave our Hearts
Hope of your blessed progress; you made it death
To stain the Marriage-bed; where shall we expect
The life of that good act, when you begin
A breach of chastitie by so black example?
If the King urge an Execution
Of what our vote, confirm'd by yours, impos'd
Upon the kingdom, you should prove your self
More innocent or give us cause to mourn
This fall from virtue

ERNESTO
Madam we grieve for you.

QUEEN
So, so, have your great wisdoms said all yet?
I laugh at you (poor things) and am so far
From trembling at your thunder, that I pitty you,
And first I'll let you know you selves, you are
I take it all my subjects, I will not
Exempt you, Sir, since Marriage takes not off
My Interest, and Essence here, all strength
Flowing from me, and your Derivative shine
Extinct, when I frown you to darkness; by
What power dare you take an accompt of me?
That am above your Laws, which must obey
Me, as their Soul, and Dye when I forsake 'em?
But I will reason coolely, and admit
They live in force; 'gainst whom? are you so shallow,
To think we that created, and decreed 'em
For vulgar reformation, must be squard
And Levell'd by 'em, as we meant to lose
Our Character and distinction, and stoop
To th' common file of subjects? this were policy!
I speak not this with sense of any guilt,
So to decline it, for I here defie you,
And bring an Innocence shall strike a blush
Upon your Souls; that sinn'd in my suspicion.

FERDINAND
Where is the Boy? Ernesto take him to
Your custodie, and bid him not despair,
I have contriv'd the rest.

[Enter **ROSANIA**, dressed as a Woman and **VIOLINDA**.

ERNESTO
He's here.

VIOLINDA
Take it upon you, if it come to searching
Wee'l find a Jurie.

CAPTAIN
You are deceiv'd my Lord, with your good pardon,
He is not here.

ERNESTO
Who is not here?

CAPTAIN
The he you do expect;
And your Officious Ladyship might well
Have spar'd your pains, to put on all this trim.

FERDINAND
What means the fellow?

CAPTAIN
'Tis no news to your Sir.
I could have told the Queen before and you
My honourable Lords, this was no Boy,
Though now he would but seem o'th' tother sex,
I knew her name.

ROSANIA
My name?

CAPTAIN
Are not you call'd Rosania?

FERDINAND
Ha! betraid?

CAPTAIN
Yes indeed is she, you were present Sir
I'th' Garden when this fine Hermophrodite
Declar'd what sex was hid behind the Breeches,
And this I certified the Prince before.

QUEEN
Now 'tis clear.

CAPTAIN

There are some tokens too I can remember,
As kisses, and excuse for marrying with
The Queen, a Virgin still, &c.

OMNES
A Woman?

VIOLINDA
But are you a Woman indeed?

CAPTAIN
And now my Lords, if you have Hearts that are
Honest and daring, come about agen,
For this is but a cunning piece of treason,
Against your Faith, and the Queens honour.

FERDINAND
We are both lost Rosania.

CAPTAIN
'Tis truth, or take my Head off.

QUEEN
You do believe this transformation,
And know this Ladie, my good Lord, I did
Suspect before the cause of your neglects,
And meeting with some dark Intelligence
From the Prince, to perfect this discovery,
Did in my Chamber woo with aptest forms
Of Love, to trie how long the sex would be
Conceal'd; you heard a part, and see us kiss,
And came in time with these wise Noblemen
To prevent further acts of shame.

RODRIGUEZ
Is't possible?

ROSANIA
It was an ill contrivement to make me
Proof of the Queens dishonour.

ERNESTO
An apparent Plot
Against the life and honour of the Queen,
Since he would urge that Law maliciously
Against her, knowing this to be a Woman,
And his close strumpet.

RODRIGUEZ
The same Law must be
Their tryall.

LEANDRO
What a change is here already?

QUEEN
You must not Lords deny me Justice.

RODRIGUEZ
'Tis insufferable
Against a common person.

ERNESTO
Let his first
Treason, if you think good Madam, be urg'd
In accusation.

LEANDRO
So, so.

QUEEN
You did us service Captain.

CAPTAIN
I am bound too't, heres more news for the Prince.

QUEEN
Use your pleasures.

[Exit.

RODRIGUEZ
What need we circumstance, let him die to morrow.

QUEEN
Death will be mercie to so much ingratitude,
Command them both to severall custodies.
The morning shall behold 'em dead—

[Exeunt all but **FERDINAND**, **ROSANIA** & **GUARD**.

ROSANIA
Now more lost then ever.

FERDINAND
Pray lets take

Short leave of one another, 'tis in vain
To reason against providence, or say
We might ha' liv'd; though I must dye, and after
Be hid in my obscurest name, and shade,
I must declare whose blood they will profane
In bleeding thee; farewell, our last, last kiss.
My heart would fain come to thee, I will make it
My humble sute with my last breath it may
Be quickly sent thee.

ROSANIA
We shall both meet, when
This dust falls off, and our souls kiss agen.

[Exeunt.

ACT V

SCENE I

The Palace.

Enter **LEANDRO, RODRIGUEZ, ERNESTO, SERVANTS** with lights.

ERNESTO
My Lord you tell us wonders, 'tis high time
To open such a mysterie.

RODRIGUEZ
This change
Will exceed all, and to convincing are
The circumstances of this great discovery
They do command our faith.

ERNESTO
And you shal steer us.

LEANDRO
Then let us lose no time; oh my good Lords,
Did you but feel the torment of my bosome,
Till I discharge the duty, which so long
Hath slept in his concealment you would call
For wings to flye, and think all motion tedious;
For Heavens sake lets make hast, that we prevent
The morning, which will rise upon this knowledge
With cheerfull beams, and put on all his glory.

ERNESTO
Most gladly we attend.

[Exeunt.

SCENE II

A Prison.

A Table and Taper set out. Enter **FERDINAND** with a book in his Hand.

FERDINAND
I have no Heart to think of any thing
But my Rosania, all devotion,
When I remember her, flyes off, and leaves
My soul no contemplation but her safety;
They were too cruel to divide us, night
It self looks now more black by this dim taper;
Rosania's eyes would brighten all; but they
Weigh'd down with sleep, and sorrow, are perhaps
At rest, a thousand Angels watch about 'em;
And let some one whose office is to wait
On harmless love, present me to her dreams;
O let her hear me often call upon her,
As I am led to death, and when the stroke
Divides me from my self, and from the World,
My Heart shall pay her tribute, and my blood
Do miracles, when every Crimson drop
My Body bleeds, shall not in vain be wept,
But fall into some Letter of her name,
To keep alive our story.

[Enter two **SERVANTS**, with torches, **LEANDRO, ERNESTO, RODRIGUEZ**.

What lights are these?
This place sure is not wont to be thus visited.
They are spirits, ha! yet if I have a memory
Those Faces were but late familiar to me.

[They Kneel.

What mockery is this? if you be substances
Of things I know, go tell the Tyrant Queen
She might allow me death without this scorn,
This jeering Antimasque.

OMNES
Long live the King.

FERDINAND
What King?

OMNES
Long live Ferdinand King of Murcia.

FERDINAND
A dream, a golden dream. What fancies wait
Upon our sleep! and yet I wake, they are
Apparitions, I'll shut my eyes, and lose 'em.
They wo not vanish. Leandro, Rodriguez, Ernesto?

OMNES
All your subjects.

LEANDRO
Collect your scatterd thoughts my Lord, and be
Assur'd, we now pay reall duties to you,
You are our King, and must be.

FERDINAND
Who says so?

LEANDRO
I, whose cold fear, and frailty,
When fate of War had made you Prisoner,
Conceal'd the truth, and Justice of your title,
'Twas I that sav'd you from your Uncles fury
And sent you to Valencia, while I cozen'd
The kingdom with your death, till time might ripen
Your challenge to the scepter; if you can
Find mercy to a treason, great as this,
I'll live, and study how to merit pardon.

FERDINAND
Rise, rise all,
And if you be Leandro, pray come neerer.

RODRIGUEZ
Pray Heav'n this unexpected happiness
Meet with no extasie, all senses are
Not arm'd for such extremes of Joy.

ERNESTO

The Queen,
When she finds this, will fall into a Feaver,
By instinct her Head must ake this very minute.

RODRIGUEZ
And shake too, for the Crown is tottering.

FERDINAND
Pardon? thou shouldst divide the kingdom with me.
But do all these believe it, will you not,
When I make second claim, deny me agen?
Call me Impostor?

LEANDRO
Sir forgive that first,
And I'l not ask Heaven pardon for my next
Deniall, let death threaten all his stings;
And I have satisfied these Lords so well,
They are confirm'd in your just claim, and person.

RODRIGUEZ and **ERNESTO**
We lay our lives and fortunes at your feet.

FERDINAND
I may command you then, fetch me Rosania;
I'll be no King without her; do not stay
To hear how much I love her 'bove the Crown,
And all the glories wait upon it, she
That was my Page, my fellow Prisoner, Rosania.

[Exit **RODRIGUEZ**

'Tis that name next to Heaven I bow too.
Good my Lord follow him, and if she be
Awake, oh drop it gently by degrees,
(The joy is mighty, she a sad weak Virgin)
That I shall live to make her Queen.

[Exit **ERNESTO**.

Stay you, and if I play too much the wanton with
My fate, or swell with expectation,
Speak something to allay my hopes, and say
There may be crosses yet, the Queen may want
Faith or consent, or put case the people
(A dangerous torrent to oppose) like not
This Innovation, where is the King then?

LEANDRO
Doubt not their Loves, you had their
Hearts before;
Let nothing shake you.

[Enter **ROSANIA, ERNESTO, RODRIGUEZ**.

FERDINAND
Th'art my better Angell.
Why then if my Rosania will be Queen,
The kingdoms ours agen; she comes, she comes.
Thou mak'st too little hast to be a Queen.
I am my self agen, my name is found,
I shall live to, thus to embrace Rosania
Without a fear, these Lords are all thy subjects,
I am a King.

LEANDRO
You are.

FERDINAND
Then what must my
Rosania be?

ROSANIA
Happy, if this be more
Than dream, my tears and sufferings are all paid for
If this be true.

LEANDRO
Most true.

ROSANIA
What a strong arm
Hath Heaven?

FERDINAND
See how the Day hath made
Hast to salute Rosania, and to wait
Upon thy triumph, blushes like a Maid
When she is told she is in Love, the Stars
Are gone to tell the other World, thy beauty,
Till now Ecclips'd with sorrow, hath thrown off
The imprisoning veil, and shines above their brightness.
But how shall we Leandro now contrive
For our Court entertainment, where the Queens
Prepar'd to hear our Tragedy?

LEANDRO
Leave me
To order your appearance; but first Sir,
We must secure this Fort.

ERNESTO
The Captain is
My creature.

FERDINAND
Thou shalt be all our direction.
Come my Rosania, time hath turn'd a gen
Our Glass, and his keen sith this comfort brings,
It cuts no scepters down but to make Kings.

[Exeunt.

SCENE III

Near the Palace.

[Enter **LEONARIO**, reading a Letter, and **SOULDIER**.

LEONARIO
So near?

SOULDIER
We heard before of your affront
My Lord, and were prepar'd.

LEONARIO
It hath outstrip'd my expectation,
These Letters say
Mendoza is their Generall new return'd
With victory from the Moores; his fame I honour,
My knowledge never reach'd his person.

SOULDIER
Sir, he brings old Soldiers with him, the
Commanders
Are such, whose faith and valor in those Wars
Already tried, he durst name to the King
To be employ'd here in your highness cause.

LEANDRO
We will to Horse immediatly. I long

To salute the Army.

SOULDIER
Which but wants your person
The Soul of their design; you may soon reach 'em.

[Enter **CAPTAIN**.

LEONARIO
I will.

CAPTAIN
Your Grace.

LEONARIO
That we had wings, away, to Horse to Horse.

[Exeunt **LEONARIO, SOULDIER**.

CAPTAIN
Speed, and you be so hot o'th' spur, my business
Is but breath, and your design it seems rides post.

[Enter **LIEUTENANT** and **ANCIENT**.

The Earth runs upon wheels; whom do I spy?
My extraordinaries, I'l ha' sport with them,
But first observe 'em.

[Walks aside.

LIEUTENANT
I see no profit in these offices
That we ha' brought.

ANCIENT
Not extraordinary, as the name did promise.

CAPTAIN
The Rogues are poor, and now repent.

ANCIENT
We were told by the cheating Captain
That we should want Men to tell our money.

LIEUTENANT
This 'tis to deal with Soldades.

ANCIENT
We should command the Ladies too, and we
Were bountiful, a small Pox take their beauties,
'Tis the greater curse, I have undone
My self in giving away enameld Rings
And Bracelets.

LIEUTENANT
Well, if I trust a Captain agen.

ANCIENT
Or I.

CAPTAIN
I'm glad they are payd; I wo'not leave 'em,
I feel my antipathy strong yet.

ANCIENT
I would venture half my soul to be reveng'd
If I knew how.

CAPTAIN
True Rascals!

LIEUTENANT
The Ladies love him.

ANCIENT
They all Love Men of War.

LIEUTENANT
Would his poop were a fire!

ANCIENT
And Battels in Bed naturally.

LIEUTENANT
Well, what Ladies give him hereafter to buy new Feathers, may his body compel him to bestow upon a Surgeon.

ANCIENT
May Diseases undermine his Flesh like Gunpowder,
And blow all his skin up into blisters.

LIEUTENANT
May they that look for his Nose, go about for want of a bridge, and let him wear no Legs but what he buyes from the Carpenter.

ANCIENT
May his face break out, and undo him in taffata, and may the patches at the last be so many, till his skin be invisible, and his goggle eyes look through a Mask.

LIEUTENANT
May he live to be as much coward as we ha' been, and be beaten!

ANCIENT
Abominably beaten, and may the miracle be on our side, that we may be valiant, and be the Men to doe it, oh I would have no more mercy.—

CAPTAIN [Coming forward]
Save you Gallants, save you Courtiers.

BOTH
My noble Captain.

ANCIENT
It may be he did not hear us.

CAPTAIN
Hark you, what purchase have you two made lately?

BOTH
Of what?

CAPTAIN
Of Lands and loggerheads, Lordships I would say, I know you are both rich, you cannot choose, But I will borrow no more o' you, faith be satisfied and leave off in time with the wealth you have.

LIEUTENANT
Where is it Captain?

ANCIENT
Can you tell where we may borrow as much money upon our extraordinary places, as will set up shop agen? For this Court trade wil' not do.

CAPTAIN
How?

LIEUTENANT
No indeed Captain, we ha' made little benefit since we came to be extraordinaries.

CAPTAIN
Ye took not the right way then.

ANCIENT
That may be.

CAPTAIN
Why, cannot you lie, and swear, and pawn your souls for six pence, the Devil could not furnish the City with two more hopeful Borachios. You have a Carrot-colour'd Beard, and that never fails, and your worships face is a prognostication of preferment
Is a Prognostication of preferment, where
Beside Dominical Letters you have all the
Conjuring Characters of the Planets.
But all this is your cunning, to dissemble your estates.

LIEUTENANT
By this empty pocket, I have but one Shirt left.

CAPTAIN
You jeast y'faith.

ANCIENT
And by all my no money, I have but half a one

CAPTAIN
Come, come, you took up linnen lately, I heard
You did.

ANCIENT
I, smocks.

CAPTAIN
Why they are in fashion with extraordinary
Courtiers.
But if you be in earnest, I can tell, where you
May furnish your selves richly.

BOTH
Where? where?

CAPTAIN
W'y in the Shops for ready money, but you would
Save charges.

ANCIENT
I marry Captain.

CAPTAIN
Venture to rob a hedge, it is but hanging,
And whats that to men extraordinary?
But if your wants be real, be not dejected,
I'll set you up agen my self, I have been
Beholding to you two for your good words

And wishes Gentlemen.

LIEUTENANT
It pleases you to say so, I begin
To smell.—

ANCIENT
Not to us Captain, we have been beholding to you.

CAPTAIN
And it happens, as if fortune had made you miserable A purpose▪ to bless you both with such a preferment, as wil' not be offerd agen in a Coronation.

LIEUTENANT
On good Captain, for we are extraordinary miserable.

CAPTAIN
Then observe; you are not ignorant how things go at Court, the King is in prison.

ANCIENT
So.

CAPTAIN
And his wench with him that walk'd in Breeches;
The Queen resolves they shall both die.

ANCIENT
Good.

CAPTAIN
This morning too; now in regard the King is a person of qualitie—

LIEUTENANT
I think he be.

CAPTAIN
And the tother a Lady, as some imagine, you two may do very well to undertake now—

BOTH
Any thing.

CAPTAIN
To be a couple of Hangmen. D'ee mark? to dispatch the Queens enemies in what horrid way, her counsell shall think convenient▪ you will do service to the State, and have extraordinary rewards; besides the honour and reputation of your places; what say? 'tis my pure love to make this first offer to you.

ANCIENT

Do we look like a couple of Hangmen?

CAPTAIN
No you ha' not so good a complexion; and now I think on't you sha' not live to have that preferment come, draw you that wear your Sword like a Bum-baliff, do as I bid you, and that quickly.

ANCIENT
It wo'not come out Sir—

CAPTAIN
No—this shall in then—

ANCIENT
I will put more strength to't.

CAPTAIN
So now, d'ee mark—kill one another.

BOTH
Kill one another?

CAPTAIN
Yes and doo't religiously, with as much alacrity as you would devour an Orphan: and do't hansomly, that you may not be hangd when you are dead. I'll see't done he that is dull shall have my goad to quicken him:—

[They fight.

So, good good agen. well offer'd—they fight by these Hilts Furiously now cou'd I forgive 'em-so, enough.

LIEUTENANT
This is very fine sport.

CAPTAIN
Necessity has taught 'em the noble science, come, if all fail, you shall fight challenges; ther's mony and broken Pates to be got that way you can make legs, and gape like Gudgeons for benevolence, cut scurvy capers, to shew your Legs are well, when your Head bleeds; farewell; stay, you want money, I had forgot, there is twelve pence apiece for you.

BOTH
How Captain? I hope not.

CAPTAIN
They are not hearty yet, they think I serve 'em with Press money agen. No, tis my pure bountie. Go, set up agen, and trust Souldiers, without impertinent asking for your debts; they'l pay you.

ANCIENT
As you ha' done.

CAPTAIN
I'l hearken how you behave you selves farewell. When you are rich, I'll visit you agen, and borrow money.

LIEUTENANT
Too much is too much: humph!

ANCIENT
Now have I a great mind to fight with your Captainship.

LIEUTENANT
So have I, now my Hands in, methinks 'tis nothing.

CAPTAIN
You are not desperate?

ANCIENT
We are a little better, as good be Hang'd for killing of you Captain, as live after the rate of our disgrace. I am resolv'd.

CAPTAIN
Two Mastiffs at once may worry me. I am put too't.

[They fight.

Must we have tother 'bout.

ANCIENT
This is enough at once we may come too't in time.

CAPTAIN
Why now I love you, love you, as well as you do Law.

ANCIENT
Upon good terms we love you too.

CAPTAIN
Let's shake Hands, you sha' not to your vomit agen. Now you dare sight, I'll tell you a hundred wayes to get moneys, come, wee'l drink and divide fortunes, Run not back into cows agen.

ANCIENT
I'll be Ancient now agen.

LIEUTENANT
And I Lieutenant.

CAPTAIN

Both my own Boyes.

ANCIENT
'Tis not so hard to fight I see, if a Man be but desperate, and give his mind to't,

LIEUTENANT
Pox a Cowards; come Captain.

CAPTAIN
Let me hug ye my brace of Myrmidons,
And drink a tun of Wine to this conversion.

[Exeunt.

SCENE IV

An Apartment in the Palace.

[Enter **QUEEN**, **VIOLINDA**.

QUEEN
The Prince so early met upon the way
This morning sayst? and with a Souldier?

VIOLINDA
And in that hast too, Madam I was told
The speed of Wings was slow, their fiery Horse
Bathing in foam, yet fled as if they meant
To leave the Wind, and Clouds behind 'em.

QUEEN
Strange!
I could have wish'd him with less discontent
To have left us, but my stubborn fate design'd it;
Having thus snatch'd away himself, it will
Become us to compose, and make the best
Of our State game; I sent a Messenger
With our command, to th' Governor of the Fort,
He should attend the King by the Water gate
Leads to the Garden, we do purpose conference;
If Ferdinand wisely consent to break
The Magick that so chains his Heart to that
Idol Rosania, wee'l be reconcil'd,
And Peace shall marry once agen our Hearts.

[Enter **COURTIER**.

Me thinks our Lords are cold in their attendance,
Where be our train of Ladies?—nay permit 'em,
A solitude becomes this sullen Day.
And our own thoughts; methinks thou dost not look
With thy own face upon me.

VIOLINDA
Not I Madam?

QUEEN
My eyes have lost their virtue, all I look on
Have not the shape and colour they presented,
What whispers that? ha'?

VIOLINDA
Here was none Madam.

QUEEN
I could be jealous of the Wind methinks,
And quarrel with the postures of those very
Shapes i'th' Arras; fie Olivia, call home thy reason.

COURTIER
O Madam!

QUEEN
What horror's in that voice? I see a treason
In's looks.

COURTIER
O Madam! I beseech your pardon.

QUEEN
Why? art a traitor?

COURTIER
Not I, but there are practices I fear
Against your royal person, the Court gates
Are shut, all's in confusion within,
And I could hear abroad loud acclamations
And triumph for the King, as he were new proclam'd.

[Enter **CAPTAIN**.

QUEEN
Which way comest thou?

CAPTAIN
Over the Wall Madam; the gates are shut,
I'll tell you news; young Ferdinand your Husband
Is in all stare attended, and proclam'd
King in his own right, he is prov'd to be
What he did first pretend himself, Leandro,
And all the Lords confirm't the Governor
Hath given him up the Fort, the wise City
Her Keys, and every officer on's knees
Is praying and drinking the Kings health,

QUEEN
Away! and let thy face be seen no more,
But when the fatall noise of fire, some blood,
Or buriall calls thee forth.

CAPTAIN
This my reward
For bringing news the King's alive? take heed,
Do not talk treason in your own defence,

[Shouts within.

—Hark

[Enter, in state, **RODRIGUEZ, ERNESTO, LEANDRO, FERDINAND**, who takes the throne, **ATTENDANTS, GUARDS** &c

QUEEN
From what an expectation am I fallen!

OMNES
Long live Ferdinand King.

FERDINAND
We thank you; and will study to be worth
Your prayers and dutie; Madam, the Chancelor
Can clear, and bring your faith to allow the wonder,
We are no Impostor now nor need we borrow
A beam from you to make us shine, yet still
You are our Cosen, fair Olivia,

[Enter **ROSANIA** and **LADIES**.

The Husband was a title long since due
To my Rosania, may it prosper here.
Our love and years grew up together, and
Our Souls by holy contract tied, when in

Alfonzo's House, her Father, and my Guardian
(To whose trust I was sent an Infant by Leandro)
We plighted faith; it is no blemish
To fair Olivia still to be a Virgin,
Though she have lost the Queen, she is a Princess.
And hath now found a Kinsman, that shall study
What shall become his love, her blood and honour.
Upon your Lip I print this fair assurance.

[Kisses the **QUEEN**.

ROSANIA
And mine shall be to do you service Madam.

QUEEN
If this be true, you must command my dutie.

FERDINAND
We hear Prince Leonario is departed,
When he shall know the progress of our fortunes
Hee'l quit his Stars, that hid their golden Heads
To mock him with a small Eclipse, o' purpose
To light him with more glorie to his happiness.

[Soft Alarm.

Ha! what clamors that? the frightfull noise increases.

[Enter **GUARD**.

GUARD
Flie, and save your selves, the Fort's surpris'd
By the Prince of Arragon, whose troups have seiz'd the
City, reeling with Wine, and careless of their strength,
In their joyes for you Sir.

FERDINAND
The Prince of Arragon? the fates cannot
Be so injust, so envious of our blessing,
To snatch it from us in a minute;

[Noise within.

Ha!

[Shouts within.
Help, help, quarter.

FERDINAND
They are i'th' Court already.

LEANDRO
We are all undone!
Lets yield and ask conditions honourable.

FERDINAND
Die he, that dares but think so yield? no, Ferdinand
Was here too late a Prisoner; let us sell
Our lives at glorious rates, the Evening puts
A Mask upon the horror, follow me.

[Exit.

LEANDRO
To certain death; Ladies stay you, the danger
Will meet us here to soon, and yet your persons
In honour challenge safety.

[Exit **LORDS**.

QUEEN
Is there no end of my distractions?
Or hath my folly yet deserv'd more vengeance?

ROSANIA
It cannot be Heaven will so soon destroy
The blessing it bestow'd if thus you punish
Whom you advance, who will believe your gifts
Are more than flattery to betray our Peace?

[Enter **LEONARIO**, **ALFONSO**, **FERDINAND**, prisoner, **RODRIGUEZ**, **ERNESTO**, **CAPTAIN**, **SOULDIERS**.

LEONARIO
This Ladie is my prize.

QUEEN
How Sir your prize?

LEONARIO
Mistake me not, ther's no dishonour meant
Your person; yet I boldly may pronounce
You are, and must be mine. I am not ignorant
You are a Virgin all but name, be wise
As you are fair, and I forget what's past,
And take this satisfaction; if I meet
Contempt, where I with honour once more Court you,

You will create a flame shall never dye
But in the Kingdoms ashes; you were mine
First by your own election, seal'd above,
If I must lose what Heaven bestow'd upon me
The quarrel is not mine
But virtues, whose right Hand is arm'd with Justice!

[Enter **CAPTAIN**.

Punish not where you owe your Heart, but let
Both our revenges meet in that Impostor;
I find your noble Soul return; Lord General
While I retire with this fair Queen, whom not
One violent accent shall affright, much less
A rude attempt, take hence that counterfeit,
And cut his Head off.

ROSANIA
O my dearest Lord?

LEONARIO
The rest may if they please find mercy.

CAPTAIN
I were best be o' this side.

LEONARIO
Away with him.

FERDINAND
Insulting Prince, thou darest not.

LEONARIO
How Sir, dare not?

FERDINAND
I said it,
Thy better, being a King, in my own right,
Without her charitie, proclam'd and justified,
By Birth a Prince.

LEANDRO
All this is truth Sir.

LEONARIO
You must not Cozen thus my faith, away;
Cut off his Head.

ALFONSO
Dispatch you with the Queen,
Let me alone to make his Head secure.

LEANDRO
Nay take mine too. I'll wait on him in death,
It shall begin my service.

ROSANIA
Cruel Prince.

QUEEN
What fate must I obey?

ROSANIA
My death will adde some lines
Unto thy bloody Chronicle; pray let us dy together.

LEONARIO
You shall speak, her sentence Madam.

QUEEN
She must live then.

LEONARIO
To all we offer mercie, but to Ferdinand,
His doom is fixt; come Madam.

QUEEN
Whither Sir?

LEONARIO
I know the way to your Chapel, he that loves us
Make hast, and bring the Priest.

[Exit **LEANDRO** and **QUEEN**.

CAPTAIN
That's I, I know
Her Chaplains, they are my friends, and all good fellows.

[Exit.

FERDINAND
Pray can you tell me, where, or what I am
Or what I must do next?

ALFONSO

Yes, you must die.

FERDINAND
Let not that grieve you Gentlemen, 'tis nothing
To part with life, and if but my Rosania would not weep
Methinks I could shake off this dust, and leap
To Immortality without a guide,
And in that cheerful flight prepare the blest
With so much praise and wonder of thy virtue,
They shall be more in love with thee, than I,
And double all their prayers to bring thee to 'em.

ROSANIA
No we will die together.

ALFONSO
You shall.

FERDINAND
How?

ALFONSO
Both live, and love, and bless my age the witness.
D'ee know me?

[Pulls off his false beard.

ROSANIA
Father?

FERDINAND
Guardian!

LEANDRO
Alfonso, my noble Kinsman.

ALFONSO
How joyes flow in my Heart, to see this constancy!

FERDINAND
How came you to be his?

ALFONSO
I have deceiv'd the Prince, our forces are Valencia's,
Not Arragons, which he by Letters sent for
In his revenge, but we met the Intelligence
And arriv'd sooner, to pretend our selves
The Armie he expected; you shall know more hereafter.

FERDINAND
I want a knowledge where to begin my gratitude,
The joyes you bring are mighty, and overcome us.
O my Rosania?

ROSANIA
This was beyond hope.

[Enter **CAPTAIN**.

CAPTAIN
So, so, 'tis done, he has mumbled up the ceremony;
A compendious Priest may do much in few words;
They are fast enough; the Queen was wise to take him;
You are onely like to be a loser Sir; they come.

[Enter **LEONARIO, QUEEN**.

ALFONSO
All joyes to the Prince of Arragon, and the fair Olivia.

LEONARIO
Why not the Queen Olivia?

ALFONSO
Not while this Gentleman's Head is on, believe it.

LEONARIO
Where is Mendoza?

ALFONSO
Hid within this bush—

[Shows his false beard.

But here's Alfonso General of the Army
Sent from Valencia to assist King Ferdinand
To his native right.

LEONARDO
Valencia?

ALFONSO
My Master having faild in his first aids
To Ferdinand, intended not sit down
With so much loss but rais'd another Army,
Which in our march consulted our security

By Interception of all passages;
Your messenger by a party was surpriz'd,
Him, stubborn to discover what he was,
Imperfect in his answer, we Interpreted
Some spie, and searching found your Letters fraught
With mischief and revenge, these sent to our King
We had command to hasten our design,
And steer our course by Sea to Carthagena,
How after we arriv'd, we gaind your faith
And purposes, Your highness knows.

LEONARIO
Betrayd!

ALFONSO
Sir, be a Prince, and just to your own honour,
And having perfected your fair desires
With her, we hope you will account your self
Most happy that you mist a power to serve
Further revenge upon a lawfull Prince.
My Soldiers will obey me now, although
To help your Marriage I appear'd no friend
To Ferdinand.

LEANDRO
Who was the Prince preserv'd
By me, and sent an Infant to this Lord,
My noble Kinsman.

ALFONSO
Him I bred, till time
And strength might arm him to return, and claim
His own.

LEONARIO
Leandro denied this before.

LEANDRO
To my dishonour, 'twas a coward fear
To lose my self unprofitably

LEONARIO
I apprehend with wonder.

FERDINAND
If you repent not love and our alliance,
She shall be worth your best embrace, and we
Forgetful of your passion, entertain you

With all affection to our blood.

LEONARIO
I meet it,
And satisfied in this story, Joy I was
Prevented; I congratulate your Stars Sir;
Nor is this treasure of less price to me
Than when her Temples were enchac'd with Empire.

QUEEN
This love will give my soul another form.

FERDINAND
Our storie hath been full of change, but love
Hath met a glorious victory, and tied
Our souls together with most firm embraces.
My Lord Leandro you shall to Valencia,
With our best thanks and greeting to the King;
His Armies charge is outs beside what else
We owe his Royall bountie. Once more welcome
Alfonso now my Father, witness I
Preserve my faith to my Rosania,
I hear the Priest call us to other rites,
His Altar doth expect another pair,
Make hast to light his Tapers with thine eyes
And make our hearts each others Sacrifice.

[Exeunt **OMNES**.

EPILOGUE

CAPTAIN
Gentlemen,
I Am no Epilogue, I come to pray
You'd tell me your opinion of the Play,
Is the Plot current? may we trust the wit
Without a Say-Master to autorise it?
Are the lines Sterling? do they hold conceit?
And every piece with your allowance, weight?
That when you come abroad, you'll not report
You are sorry to have given white money for't?
So, so, I know your meaning, now pray tell
How did the action please ye, was it well?
How did King Stephen do, and tother Prince?
Enough, enough, I apprehend, and since
I am at questions w'ee, tell me faith

How do you like the Captain? Ha! he saith,
I'l tell you, y' are my friends, none here, he knows,
I mean you o' the Gentry, t'whom he owes
No money, will enter a false action,
And let the rest look too't, if there be one,
Among his City creditors, that dares,
He hath vow'd to press, and send him to the Wars.

JAMES SHIRLEY – A CONCISE BIBLIOGRAPHY

The following includes years of first publication, and of performance if known, together with dates of licensing by the Master of the Revels if available.

TRAGEDIES
The Maid's Revenge (licensed 9th February 1626; printed, 1639)
The Traitor (licensed 4th May 1631; printed, 1635)
Love's Cruelty (licensed 14th November 1631; printed, 1640)
The Politician (acted, 1639; printed, 1655)
The Cardinal (licensed 25th May 1641; printed, 1652).

TRAGI-COMEDIES
The Grateful Servant (licensed 3rd November 1629 as The Faithful Servant; printed 1630)
The Young Admiral (licensed 3rd July 1633; printed 1637)
The Coronation (licensed 6th February 1635, as Shirley's, but printed in 1640 as a work of John Fletcher)
The Duke's Mistress (licensed 18th January 1636; printed 1638)
The Gentleman of Venice (licensed 30th October 1639; printed 1655)
The Doubtful Heir (printed 1652), licensed as Rosania, or Love's Victory in 1640
The Imposture (licensed 10th November 1640; printed 1652)
The Court Secret (printed 1653).

COMEDIES
Love Tricks, or the School of Complement (licensed 10th February 1625; printed under its subtitle, 1631)
The Wedding (ca. 1626; printed 1629)
The Brothers (licensed 4th November 1626; printed 1652)
The Witty Fair One (licensed 3rd October 1628; printed 1633)
The Humorous Courtier (licensed 17th May 1631; printed 1640).
The Changes, or Love in a Maze (licensed 10th January 1632; printed 1639)
Hyde Park (licensed 20th April 1632; printed 1637)
The Ball (licensed 16th November 1632; printed 1639)
The Bird in a Cage, or The Beauties (licensed 21st January 1633; printed 1633)
The Gamester (licensed 11th November 1633; printed 1637)
The Example (licensed 24th June 1634; printed 1637)
The Opportunity (licensed 29th November 1634; printed 1640)
The Lady of Pleasure (licensed 15th October 1635; printed 1637)
The Royal Master (acted and printed 1638)
The Constant Maid, or Love Will Find Out the Way (printed 1640)

The Sisters (licensed 26th April 1642; printed 1653).
Honoria and Mammon (printed 1659)

DRAMAS
A Contention for Honor and Riches (printed 1633), morality play
The Triumph of Peace (licensed 3rd February 1634; printed 1634), masque
The Arcadia (printed 1640), pastoral tragicomedy
St. Patrick for Ireland (printed 1640), neo-miracle play
The Triumph of Beauty (ca. 1640; printed 1646), masque
The Contention of Ajax and Ulysses (printed 1659), entertainment
Cupid and Death (performed 26th March 1653; printed 1659), masque

www.ingramcontent.com/pod-product-compliance
Lightning Source LLC
Chambersburg PA
CBHW071312060426
42444CB00034B/1975